Merrimack Valley MEMORIES

Volume III - The 1940s, '50s & '60s

ACKNOWLEDGMENTS

The Eagle-Tribune is pleased to present Merrimack Valley Memories Vol. III, The 1940s, '50s & '60s. It must be noted, however, that this unique pictorial history book would not have been possible without the generous contributions made by many people from virtually every corner of our valley.

We are indebted, first of all, to those early Merrimack Valley residents who captured their time—our history—in photographs, and provided a glimpse into their lives.

Secondly, all Merrimack Valley residents are indebted to the many individuals who are committed to preserving our history in various libraries, historical societies, history centers, archives and personal collections throughout our valley.

Project Coordinator - Linda A. Gardner
Editor - Al White
Advertising Director - Tim Brady
Publisher - Al Getler

The following organizations and collectors have contributed greatly to this project:

Andover Historical Society　　　　　**Joseph Bella, The Bella Collection**
North Andover Historical Society　　　　　**Plaistow Historical Society**
Haverhill Public Library Special Collections　　　　　**Salem Historical Society**
Lawrence History Center　　　　　**Stevens Memorial Library in North Andover**
Lawrence Public Library

Published by Pediment Publishing, a division of The Pediment Group, Inc. www.pediment.com

FOREWORD

IF YOU GREW UP IN THE MERRIMACK VALLEY IN THE 1940S, '50S OR '60S, YOU'RE LIKELY TO FIND THE FACES OF people you know in this book. You may even find your own face here.

This is the third volume in our "Merrimack Valley Memories" series. Inside you'll find more than 325 photographs from the decades when the baby boom generation was born, grew up and came of age.

There are thousands of faces here.

Were you a paperboy for The Evening Tribune in the 1950s? Maybe you're in the photo of the flock of carriers picking up their bundles at Willow and Park streets in Lawrence.

Recognize anyone in the photo of Haverhill High students at an early 1950s football game? There's a future mayor in the group. Maybe you were there, too.

Do you sill think fondly of summer days at Drummond Playground in North Andover or those mackerel fishing trips with your dad aboard Eastman's out of Seabrook?

There all here.

Even more than the first two volumes, this book is about the people of the Merrimack Valley and Southern New Hampshire. It's about how we looked, dressed, worked and played.

And it's especially about the young people of those eras, the ones who went off to war in the 1940s and the children they raised in the 1950s and '60s.

It's about the Cub Scout packs and Little League teams, the high school marching bands and cheerleading squads, the dances and parades, graduations and proms.

We thank our sponsors who made this book possible and the local historical societies, collectors and ordinary residents who shared their treasured images and family photo albums with us.

We hope you enjoy pouring over the photos and recalling those times, people and places as much as we enjoyed putting this book together.

Al White
Editor
The Eagle-Tribune

NORTHERN ESSEX COMMUNITY COLLEGE IS PROUD TO CALL THE MERRIMACK VALLEY HOME.

We have campuses in Haverhill and Lawrence, and the great majority of our students, faculty, and staff live in this beautiful area.

In addition, most of the 33,000 graduates of the college are employed locally, as, health care professionals, business owners, police officers, educators, accountants and lawyers, and more.

Ask anyone in the Merrimack Valley about his or her connection to the college, and it is likely he or she is a graduate or has a family member, close friend, co-worker or neighbor who attended the college.

At NECC, community is at the center of who we are and all that we do. It is our honor and privilege to sponsor this fascinating book covering the Merrimack Valley's rich history.

Lane A. Glenn
President

TABLE OF CONTENTS

The 1940s 7

The 1950s 55

The 1960s 109

Business Profiles 135

Index 141

CHAPTER ONE

THE 1940s

THE 1940s REPRESENT ALMOST THE LAST MYTHICAL DECADE in American life. These were the final years before television almost completely reshaped American life, and it was a time most Americans either remember or think of as the age of a small-town, country way of living. It is also a decade defined by almost two opposite extremes: a time of romanticism and innocence clashing with warfare and a seismic shift in the global political landscape.

It was romantic, certainly, but then there is the photo of the group of young men, full of confidence and life, standing on the platform at the Lawrence Railroad Depot in May of 1942 heading off to a conflict they may still have known little about.

Look at the young people on page 23 dismantling that old jalopy in Andover in 1943 to salvage parts for the war effort. It was still largely a time when you personally knew many young men who had gone off to war. It was a time of USO dances and War Bond drives.

It was the last decade captured almost exclusively in black and white. Movies, for the most part, were not in color. TV - what there was of it - was in grainy black and white. Your home photographs and the magazines delivered to your door were etched in black and white. Color was for special occasions.

There was still a commingling of the old and the new. The four men standing in front of the truck in Lawrence rallying for President Franklin D. Roosevelt are wearing top hats and long coats and could easily be situated in an image from the late 1800s. Many of the old traditions were still part of American life.

The 1940s may be very quickly fading away from living memory (it was an era that dawned now more than 70 years ago). But seeing the images on the following pages also come with a soundtrack. We can hear, if we close our eyes, the music played by the Murach Brothers Orchestra in Lawrence. We can still hear, faintly, the clacking of the typewriters in the old Eagle-Tribune newsroom on Essex Street in Lawrence in 1940. These sounds have not gone away.

It was a time when air travel was relatively new and local. When planes were remarkably uncomfortable and yet still had that sleek industrial design that foreshadowed the sleeker machines that were still to come. It was an era when science fiction writing was entering the mainstream, and children were looking to the Moon and Mars and beyond for signs of life.

This was a time of big white-walled tires and heavy metal American cars with names like Pontiac and Ford and Chrysler and Packard. The 1940s. It was a time, all right.

— Lars Trodson

OPPOSITE: Communities in the Merrimack Valley got behind War Bond efforts during World War II. This photo was taken in Andover.
COURTESY ANDOVER HISTORICAL SOCIETY

RIGHT: The Murach Brothers Orchestra, a premier polka band that appeared regularly on radio station WLAW and at polka festivals throughout New England and local dance halls. William Chaff, Sr., is the marimba player. Photo taken at the Polish Home on Brook Street in Lawrence, 1940. COURTESY WILLIAM H. CHAFF JR.

ABOVE: Arlington Mills Band of Lawrence at the New York World's Fair in 1940.
COURTESY JOSEPH BELLA COLLECTION

RIGHT: Official publicity photo for the Tony Brown Orchestra, circa 1940. The orchestra played at ballrooms all over New England for nearly 40 years. The group was formed by the three Barone brothers of Lawrence. Tony Barone is seated. Tico is third from the right and Joe is fourth from the right. COURTESY LISA (BARONE) BERNARD

ABOVE: Americo A. Petteruti, of Lawrence, was the first recruit at the opening of the Lowell enlistment station at the age of 19. He enlisted in the Air Corps for service in Panama on August 23, 1940. His son, Anthony, joined the Navy and served on the USS Dickson in the 1970s. Americo retired in October 1979 as Chief Petty Officer. COURTESY AMERICO AND JOSEPHINE PETTERUTI

TOP LEFT: Interior of Haverhill High School library, circa 1940. COURTESY HAVERHILL PUBLIC LIBRARY

LEFT: The Eagle-Tribune newsroom, circa 1940. At the middle desk in the middle row is Walter J. Coleman. COURTESY NANCY MARCOUX

ABOVE: Assembling candy vending machine at Arthur H. DuGrenier Co. at 15 Hale Street, Haverhill, circa 1940. COURTESY HAVERHILL PUBLIC LIBRARY

OPPOSITE: Rally for Roosevelt in Lawrence, 1940. COURTESY LAWRENCE HISTORY CENTER

BELOW: Wood Mill presentations by Angela Scire and friends, Lawrence, 1940. COURTESY NATALIE MELISI

ABOVE: View of the YMCA Building in Lawrence, 1940. COURTESY LAWRENCE HISTORY CENTER

RIGHT: American Legion Hall on Franklin Street, Lawrence, 1940. COURTESY LAWRENCE HISTORY CENTER

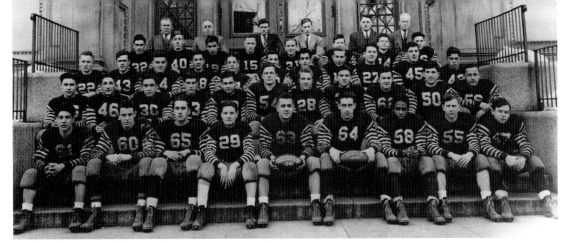

ABOVE: Lawrence High School football team of 1940-41. COURTESY LAWRENCE HISTORY CENTER

LEFT: Lawrence-born, New England Light Heavyweight Champion Arthur Flynn, left, poses with Lawrence-born, New England Lightweight Champion Andy Callahan, circa 1940. COURTESY LAWRENCE HISTORY CENTER

RIGHT: St. Anthony's Church CYO baseball team, city champs in 1939, 1940 and 1941, taken on the steps of the church at 268 Elm St. in Lawrence. Top row, from left: coach Charles Zraket, Edward Harb, Edward Hatem, John Hashem, manager Abe Beshara. Middle row: Edward Jowdy, Sam Antoon, Tony Touma, Edmond Solomon. Bottom row: Lenny Ramey, Fred Ead, Joe Assad, Joe Touma, Scotty Gabriel. COURTESY SALEM HISTORICAL SOCIETY

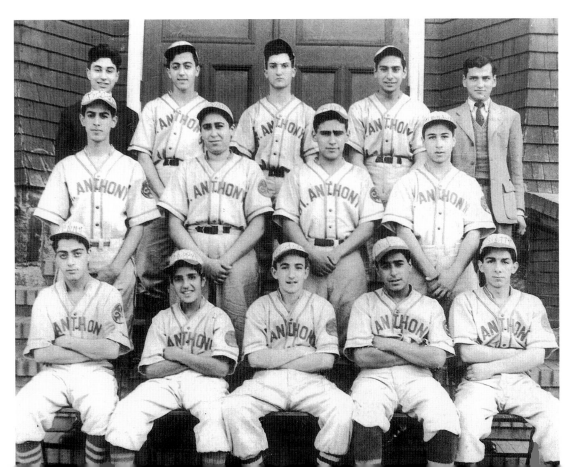

ABOVE: Holy Rosary School May Procession, circa 1941. May Queen was Dr. Rose Scuderi. Her attendants were Sarah Russo, Catherine Catalano DeBurro, Josephine Fisichella, Constance Fisichella, Josephine Mangione Brooks and Mary Messina. COURTESY KAY CATALANO DEBURRO

TOP LEFT: John Salafia's wedding at Holy Rosary Church in Lawrence, 1942. Joseph Scire was the usher. COURTESY NATALIE MELISI

LEFT: Holy Rosary School May Procession, Summer Street, Lawrence, May 14, 1941. Josephine Garofalo Petteruti, left, with Annmarie Garofalo Panorelli. COURTESY JOSEPHINE GAROFALO PETTERUTI

RIGHT: North Andover unit of the Massachusetts State Guard in the fall of 1941. It was later named the 26th Company of the 24th Infantry of the Massachusetts State Guard. COURTESY HARRY THOMAS

ABOVE: A submarine was brought into Lawrence in the early 1940s as part of a War Bond drive. The submarine is in front of the Eagle-Tribune Building on Essex Street. COURTESY LILLIAN TOOHEY

LEFT: Army Pvt. Harold Anderson and his wife Alberta, Boxford Street, Lawrence, 1942. COURTESY SANDRA KANNHEISER

ABOVE: Men departing for the Army at Lawrence Railroad Depot, (Boston & Maine Railroad station on Merrimack Street), May 12, 1942. Jerry Guilmette is kneeling, far right. COURTESY THE GUILMETTE FAMILY

LEFT: Poster of Air Show in Haverhill, June 29, 1941. COURTESY DAVE DUTTON

FAR LEFT: Pilot Howard Dutton, right, in front of Waco Cabin biplane, 1940s. COURTESY DAVE DUTTON

ABOVE: Jerry Guilmette on leave with Connie Fairweather and Kay Guilmette in front of his home at 50 Mt. Vernon Street, Lawrence, 1942. THE GUILMETTE FAMILY

RIGHT: The Scire family, Lawrence, 1942. In the photo are World War II veteran Salvatore, Angela, Joseph, Sam and Connie. COURTESY NATALIE MELISI

OPPOSITE: "Night with Robert Burns" at United Presbyterian Church in Lawrence, 1942. Robert Burns' birthday was a yearly celebration among the Scottish. Middle row, third from left: Minister Archibald Mac Millan, Grace Innes, to his right. COURTESY BARBARA INNES

LEFT: Review stand during the Lawrence Fourth of July Parade in 1942.
COURTESY LAWRENCE PUBLIC LIBRARY

BOTTOM LEFT: Lawrence Fourth of July Parade in 1942.
COURTESY LAWRENCE PUBLIC LIBRARY

OPPOSITE: Thwaites Market at the corner of Railroad Street and Oakland Avenue in Methuen, circa 1942. In front of the store are Thomas Thwaite, left, and his brother Charles Thwaite.
COURTESY JOSEPH BELLA COLLECTION

BELOW: Lawrence Fourth of July Parade in 1942.
COURTESY LAWRENCE PUBLIC LIBRARY

ABOVE: Block party in Lawrence, September 21, 1943.
COURTESY LAWRENCE PUBLIC LIBRARY/CRONIN COLLECTION

RIGHT: Angela Scire, Grace Balsamo Mistretta and Nellie Balsamo at Pleasant Valley Farm in Methuen, 1942. COURTESY NATALIE MELISI

FAR RIGHT: Three-alarm fire swept through the Merrimack Ice Co. houses on Round Pond, also known as Pentucket Lake, in Haverhill, July 20, 1942.
COURTESY HAVERHILL PUBLIC LIBRARY

ABOVE: Lawrence Postmaster Cronin with French sailors at Capri Cafe in Lawrence, October 1, 1943.
COURTESY LAWRENCE PUBLIC LIBRARY/CRONIN COLLECTION

ABOVE: A view of the post office in Lawrence, circa 1943. COURTESY LAWRENCE PUBLIC LIBRARY/CRONIN COLLECTION

LEFT: Lawrence Postmaster Charles Cronin inaugurates a war bond drive at Ayer Mills during World War II.
COURTESY LAWRENCE PUBLIC LIBRARY/CRONIN COLLECTION

TOP: St. Anne's Drum Corps performing at a war bonds rally at the post office in Lawrence in the early 1940s. COURTESY LAWRENCE PUBLIC LIBRARY/CRONIN COLLECTION

BOTTOM LEFT: War Bond event in Lawrence to raise funds for World War II, circa 1943. In the photo are Mrs. Claudia Meehan, mayor's wife; actress Dorothy Lamour; Mayor James Meehan; Edward Callahan, superintendent of schools; Jack Melincoff, theatre manager; and John O'Hearn, newspaperman (managing editor of the Eagle Tribune). COURTESY LAWRENCE HISTORY CENTER

BOTTOM RIGHT: World War II Lawrence servicemen and their dates attend a function at the Boys Club. USO volunteer hostesses, the 'Victory Belles,' are Grace Boediner McColbe and Gertrude Breen Dwyer. COURTESY LAWRENCE HISTORY CENTER

OPPOSITE: Youth dismantle a car for metal parts to aid with war efforts during World War II, Andover, circa 1943. COURTESY ANDOVER HISTORICAL SOCIETY

RIGHT: David Tinkham and his sister Patricia, ages 6 and 4 respectively, at 6 Lawrence Street in Methuen, July 1944. COURTESY DAVID J. TINKHAM

FAR RIGHT: Rollins School sixth-grade students celebrate end-of-year with a party, Lawrence, 1943. Front row, from left: Justine Lynch, unidentified, Peter Siccerrollis, Ronald Bramhill, Robert Hien, Andrew Puglessi, Alberta Earley. Middle row: Dan Menihan, Alan Hay, unidentified, unidentified, Gloria Fisichelli. Back row: unidentified, Ray Monroe, Anthony Tessitore, Barbara Borelli, Ruth Luistro, Anne Raineri, two unidentified, Billy Klien. COURTESY FRANK BAGGETT

ABOVE: Windham Center School, third-grade students, 1943. Pictured are John McGowan, Frank Johnson, Joanne Jones, Ruth Dean, Leila Phelps, Dolores Graham, Roland Jacobs and Robert Rioux. COURTESY MARY T. JOHNSON

LEFT: Kay Guilmette enjoying a drive in a Pontiac at 50 Mt. Vernon Street, Lawrence, 1943. COURTESY THE GUILMETTE FAMILY

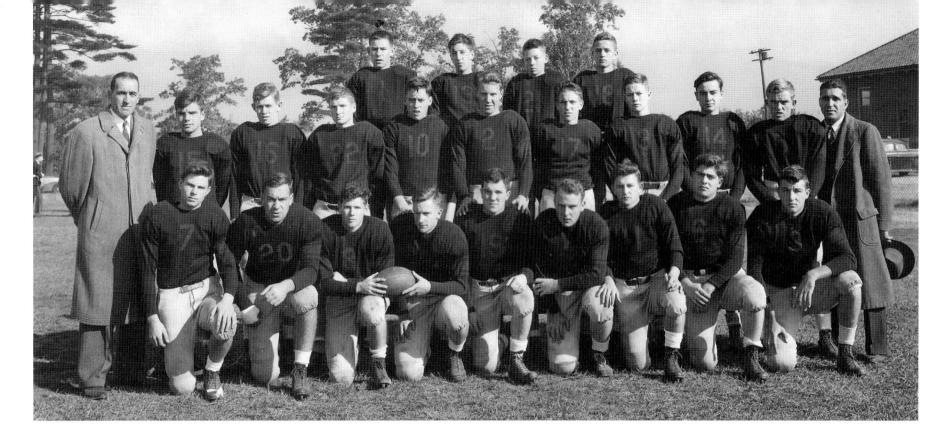

ABOVE: North Andover's Johnson High School 1943 football team at the stadium in Lawrence. First row, from left: Stewart Wilson, Bob Olenio, Phil Long and Nick Evangelos. Second row: Coach George (Benny) Lee, Georgie (Babe) Casale, G. Lefty Thomas, Jack Eilkerson, Tom Crabtree, Mike Neketuk, Harold Vincent, Dougie Lee, Jack Canty, Jack Sullivan, Coach Jim Cavileri (Cav). Third row: Reid Norris, Paul Hulub, Don Rennie, Ray Sullivan, Johnnie Cyr, Jackie Poh, Jackie Doherty, Gasper Balsamo, Tommy Gosselin. COURTESY ALMA LONG

LEFT: Lawrence Boys Club baseball team, 1943. Front row, from left: Joseph DeMonaco, Michael Nardone, Frank Annaldo, Al Borelli, Phillip Nardone. Back row: John Ianazzo, Emil Vitale, Roland Trignani, William Condurelli, Carl DeBurro. COURTESY CARMINE DEMONACO

RIGHT: Gertrude P. Ashe and James I. Meehan walk down the aisle after their marriage ceremony at St. Mary's Church in Lawrence in 1944. Lieutenant James I. Meehan was the son of Lawrence Mayor James P. Meehan. COURTESY DAVID MEEHAN

ABOVE: Santa 'Sally' 'Babes' Sapia Garofalo and Domenic 'Dick' 'Garry' Garofalo of Lawrence on their wedding day at Holy Rosary Church, April 30, 1944. COURTESY JOANNE GAROFALO EARLEY

LEFT: Jeannette Cordeau and James F. Baggett on their wedding day, Lawrence, 1944. They were married at St. Augustine Church, Tower Hill, August 20, 1944. James, a torpedoman, third class, served on a PT boat in the Pacific Theater. COURTESY FRANK BAGGETT

OPPOSITE: St. Mary's Boy Scout Troop, Lawrence, 1945. COURTESY LAWRENCE HISTORY CENTER

100%
BOYS' LIFE
1945

RIGHT TOP: Pilot Howard Dutton alongside his Boeing F4 B4 in Haverhill, 1940s. COURTESY DAVE DUTTON

RIGHT BOTTOM: Sacred Heart, Lawrence, classroom in the 1940s. COURTESY JOSEPH BELLA COLLECTION

BELOW: Ella Basso of Basso's Fancy Fruit and Candy Store on Main Street in Andover, circa 1945. Ella had to close the store due to health reasons in the late 1940s. COURTESY JO-ANN BASSO

ABOVE: A large group poses in front of Stevens Mill in North Andover, circa 1945.
COURTESY LOUISE LAMPREY FITZGERALD

LEFT: Haverhill High School graduates Ames Carroll and Barbara Atkins, June 1945.
COURTESY BARBARA ATKINS

FAR LEFT: Michael Petteruti, usher and maintenance man for Capital Theater, 1940s. The theater was on Common Street in Lawrence.
COURTESY AMERICO AND JOSEPHINE PETTERUTI

RIGHT: Nellie Barker making tabbouleh at a picnic in Lawrence, 1940s.
COURTESY LENA M. BISTANY-NYE

FAR RIGHT: Peter Minicucci with his tuba in the 1940s. Peter played in bands throughout the Merrimack Valley.
COURTESY HARRY THOMAS

BELOW: 'Nite Club' at the YMCA canteen in Lawrence, 1945. Bus fare and refreshments were provided for servicemen.
COURTESY LAWRENCE PUBLIC LIBRARY

ABOVE: Bernice Bryant Downs was a member of the 1946 Punchard High School Band, shown here in front of Andover's WWI Auditorium. COURTESY BERNICE BRYANT DOWNS

OPPOSITE: Boy Scouts march in a parade in Andover during the 1940s. COURTESY ANDOVER HISTORICAL SOCIETY

ABOVE: Group of Lawrence Junior USO hostesses, circa 1945.
COURTESY LAWRENCE PUBLIC LIBRARY

LEFT: Junior USO girls at United Formal in July, 1945.
COURTESY LAWRENCE PUBLIC LIBRARY

OPPOSITE: A group of youngsters, possibly from St. Ann's Home in Methuen, enjoy an outing at the Lawrence Stadium in the 1940s, complete with a Coca-Cola. COURTESY LAWRENCE HISTORY CENTER

RIGHT TOP: Aerial view of Lawrence, 1940s.
COURTESY LAWRENCE PUBLIC LIBRARY

RIGHT BOTTOM: Aerial view of Lawrence in the 1940s featuring the railroad yards and the David Brown Company.
COURTESY JOSEPH BELLA COLLECTION

BELOW: A 1940s postcard featuring Bon Secours Hospital in Methuen.
COURTESY JOSEPH BELLA COLLECTION

BOTTOM LEFT: A view of Plaistow in the 1940s.
COURTESY PLAISTOW HISTORICAL SOCIETY

LEFT: Merrimack National Bank at the corner of Merrimack Street and West Street, Haverhill, 1940s. This photo was taken after completion of renovations at the bank. COURTESY HAVERHILL PUBLIC LIBRARY

BOTTOM LEFT: Main Street in Salem, westbound at Salem Depot, 1940s. At present this is the intersection of NH Routes 28 and 97. COURTESY SALEM HISTORICAL SOCIETY

ABOVE: Andover decorated for Christmas in the 1940s. This view is Main Street. COURTESY ANDOVER HISTORICAL SOCIETY

ABOVE: Family-owned custom-made furniture slipcover business advertisement on front door of home owned by Santa 'Sally' 'Babes' Sapia Garofalo and Domenic 'Dick' 'Gary' Garofalo. The home was at 73 Garden Street (now General Street), Lawrence, 1946. COURTESY JOANNE GAROFALO EARLEY

RIGHT TOP: Don Sully's Swingsters starring Sally DiPaolo at a performance in Lawrence, 1946. COURTESY JO BALSAMO DIPAOLO

RIGHT BOTTOM: Methuen High School Band in 1946. COURTESY JOSEPH BELLA COLLECTION

ABOVE: Andover World War II veterans class, Punchard High School, October 1946. They are standing on the steps of the Memorial Auditorium. COURTESY JOHN PETTY

LEFT: Pfc. Gilbert N. Atkins picking up his dog, Whitey, at Railway Express Agency in Haverhill, January 1946. He got her in Naples, Italy in 1944 and took her with him throughout the war in Europe. Upon his discharge, he paid $72.65 to have her shipped home. Whitey lived 16 years. COURTESY BARBARA ATKINS

ABOVE: South Church Men's Club auction, Andover, 1947. COURTESY ANDOVER HISTORICAL SOCIETY

RIGHT: Harry F. Robinson with his pet chicken, Plaistow, circa 1947. Harry lived at 7 Elm Street. He is standing in the driveway to his home. The back side of the Town Hall is in the distance. COURTESY PLAISTOW HISTORICAL SOCIETY

ABOVE: Joe Mailloux and his brother-in-law Arthur Sirois in front of a wooden lion carved by Arthur's father Honore Sirois. A story ran in the February 23, 1940, edition of the Eagle-Tribune about a meter reader that mistook the wooden lion for a real one and came running out of Mr. Sirois' basement. COURTESY DONNA MAILLOUX

ABOVE: The intersection of Main and Chestnut streets in Andover, circa 1946. COURTESY ANDOVER HISTORICAL SOCIETY

RIGHT: Main Street looking north, Andover, May 1946. Photo was taken from Andover Savings Bank roof. On the left are Miller's Shoe Repair, Bendix Laundry, Rod Hill's Hardware. The right side shows Hood's Creamery, Barnard Insurance, Town Hall Building, Dalton's Pharmacy, Barnard Building and Musgrove Building in the background COURTESY ANDOVER HISTORICAL SOCIETY

FAR RIGHT: W.T. Grant Building at 42-54 Merrimack Street, Haverhill, October 31, 1947. COURTESY HAVERHILL PUBLIC LIBRARY

LEFT: Mr. Bedard, Donat 'Joe' Mailloux, Arthur Sirois and Donat Laroche in front of Bedard and Laroche Grocery Store at the corner of Inman and Brookfield streets in South Lawrence, circa 1947. Joe Mailloux later opened Mailloux's Market on the corner of Weare Street and South Broadway.
COURTESY DONNA MAILLOUX

BOTTOM LEFT: Aerial view of Andover in 1947.
COURTESY ANDOVER HISTORICAL SOCIETY

BELOW: Aerial view of Shawsheen Village, circa 1947.
COURTESY ANDOVER HISTORICAL SOCIETY

RIGHT: Bolta Company baseball team, Greater Lawrence baseball champions in 1947. Front row, from left: Arthur Rogers, Max Bishop, Edmund Ordzie, John Kobos, John 'Pat' Henneley, Ralph Rhodes, Joseph Korsak. Back row: Manager William F. Botsch, John McCarthy, Chester Piskadlo, William Beaudoin, Arthur Mawson, Frank McAvoy, Assistant Manager Fred Sapienza.
COURTESY JOSEPH BELLA COLLECTION

BELOW: Sandlot football team, the Howard Rams, at Juniper Street Park in Lawrence, circa 1947. Front row, from left: Bob Garvey, Carl Dequattro, Philip Burns, Bob Pierce, Jack Sheehy. Back row: Jim Sheehy, David Tinkham, Bob Silva, Bill Tinkham.
COURTESY DAVID J. TINKHAM

ABOVE: Plaistow Boys Athletic Basketball team, 1946-47. Kneeling, from left: Leo Doyon, Dick Trombley, Don Clement, Norman Mercier, Bob Trombley. Standing: Bob Rochussen, Jerry Doyon, Ray 'Shorty' Doyon, Rod Moore, Maurice 'Jake' Collins. COURTESY PLAISTOW HISTORICAL SOCIETY

ABOVE: St. Joseph's Grammar School graduation class, Haverhill, 1948. Back row, on left is Rachel Cormier. COURTESY LINDA GARDNER

LEFT: Professor Joseph Pulvina's orchestra, a popular group in Lawrence, circa 1948.
COURTESY LOUISE LAMPREY FITZGERALD

BELOW: Program at First Methodist Church in North Andover, 1948. COURTESY SHIRLEY A WILSON

ABOVE: American Legion Post 219, North Andover, circa 1948. COURTESY HARRY THOMAS

TOP RIGHT: Lawrence General Hospital School of Nursing students, 1949. Front row, from left: Muriel Jellison, Frances Schoenfeld, Barbara Johnson, Virginia Hart, Dorothy Conradsen, Bertha Trumbull, Esther Friedrich. Second row: Harriet Beek, R.N.; Beverly Howard, Lorice Mansour, Arlene Ramskill, Doris Rancourt, Shirley Kelly, Nellie Pupillo. Back row: Gloria Lavigne, Constance Duggan, Catherine Murphy, Cornelia Murphy, Alma Sanford, Eileen Greenwood, Evelyn Johnson. COURTESY ALMA LONG

RIGHT: Carmela Pennisi washing dishes with her son Sam Pennisi at Pleasant Valley Farm in Methuen, 1948. COURTESY MAUREEN TOOHEY-CURLEYO

FAR RIGHT: John Michael Hideriotis making doughnuts at Tasty Fine Do-Nut Company on Cedar Street in Haverhill, circa 1948. COURTESY HAVERHILL PUBLIC LIBRARY

LEFT TOP: Harry S. Truman speaks to a crowd during a campaign stop in Lawrence in 1948. On left is John J. Buckley, who was elected mayor of Lawrence three years later. COURTESY LAWRENCE HISTORY CENTER

LEFT BOTTOM: Harry S. Truman speaks to the crowd during a campaign stop in Lawrence, 1948. From left, first row are Gov. Paul Dever, Harry S. Truman, Congressman Thomas Lane and Margaret Truman. COURTESY LAWRENCE HISTORY CENTER

BELOW: Warren Greenwood at the WHAV microphone in Haverhill, June 1948. COURTESY HAVERHILL PUBLIC LIBRARY

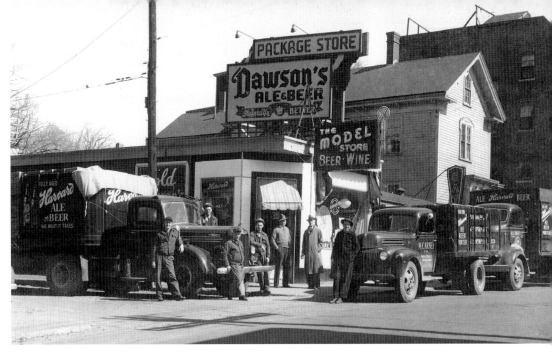

ABOVE: The Model Store, package store for beer and wine, at the corner of White and Auburn streets, Haverhill, 1940s. COURTESY HAVERHILL PUBLIC LIBRARY

ABOVE: Baptist Church on Essex Street in Andover, circa 1948.
COURTESY ANDOVER HISTORICAL SOCIETY

RIGHT: Tailoring department at Elander's Men's Shop, circa 1949.
COURTESY ANDOVER HISTORICAL SOCIETY

LEFT: Ground-breaking ceremony for the Mt. Vernon Veterans Housing Project in Lawrence, circa 1949. The Lawrence City Council was on hand for the event as was Mayor James P. Meehan, seen holding the shovel. COURTESY DAVID MEEHAN

BELOW: Dedication of the WWII statue on the Lawrence Common in 1949. Mayor James P. Meehan acted as master of ceremonies for the event. The bronze memorial was created by the same artist that sculpted the Gloucester Fisherman. COURTESY DAVID MEEHAN

RIGHT: Dorothy and Joan Keezer dressed in period clothing to celebrate Plaistow's Bicentennial in 1949.
COURTESY PLAISTOW HISTORICAL SOCIETY

OPPOSITE: A humorous entry in Plaistow's 200th anniversary parade in 1949.
COURTESY PLAISTOW HISTORICAL SOCIETY

BELOW: Plaistow fire apparatus was part of the Bicentennial parade in 1949.
COURTESY PLAISTOW HISTORICAL SOCIETY

ABOVE: Group poses for the Bicentennial celebration in Plaistow, 1949. Kneeling are Phyllis Landry and Joan Keezer. Seated are Gloria LeClair, June Edson, Evelyn Wilson, Cynthia McKewen, Pauline Legge, Ginny LeClair and Mary Gilman. Standing are Beulah Landry, Dorothy Keezer, Bernice Glover, David Ladd, Louis Heil, Doris Heil, Jean Moore, Ada Veroneau and Liz Brown. COURTESY PLAISTOW HISTORICAL SOCIETY

BELOW: Plaistow's Bicentennial, children's parade in 1949.
COURTESY PLAISTOW HISTORICAL SOCIETY

ABOVE: South Church Alpha Phi Chi Sorority Past Presidents' Night in Andover, October 6, 1949. Front row, from left: Gladys Hill, Madeline Mondale, Harriet Newman and Louise Sherman. Back row, from left: Irene Collins, May Elander, Ruth Godfrey, Mrs. Robert Hatton, Dorothy Munroe and Edith McCollum.
COURTESY ANDOVER HISTORICAL SOCIETY

TOP RIGHT: Connie Bella standing in front of her new house at 46 Fulton Street in Lawrence with her two children, Joe, left, and Angela, circa 1949.
COURTESY JOSEPH BELLA COLLECTION

RIGHT: Punchard High School football team, Andover, 1949.
COURTESY ANDOVER HISTORICAL SOCIETY

ABOVE: View of Main Street at White's Corner, Haverhill, 1949.
COURTESY HAVERHILL PUBLIC LIBRARY

TOP LEFT: Group of students cross Water Street at White's Corner, Haverhill, 1949.
COURTESY HAVERHILL PUBLIC LIBRARY

LEFT: Smith Chevrolet Co. at 76-88 Main Street, Haverhill, circa 1949. COURTESY HAVERHILL PUBLIC LIBRARY

CHAPTER TWO

THE 1950s

THE 1950S WAS THE AGE OF CINERAMA. EVERYTHING GOT BIG IN THE 1950s. The cars got big. Dresses got big. The movies got big, and the ambitions of a country and its people got very big, indeed. The 1950s in America was not the staid, quiet, conformist decade that some have tried to portray it as. That was the 1950s that was being portrayed on TV, on "The Honeymooners" or "Leave It To Beaver" or "Ozzie and Harriet."

No, no. The 1950s was a bustling, jumping time, when the American vernacular was leaning toward jazz and modern poetry, and movies were getting more daring — when words that no one thought they would ever hear on the screen were beginning to creep in. The very young men, and many young women, who had come home from the war had gotten a little older, were settling down, and starting to run businesses and lead the country into the new decade.

There was war, of course. The short, nasty Korean War. As devastating as that was to many, by 1952 Americans were electing a new president in Dwight Eisenhower and trying their best to move on.

Move on they did. It was the decade when the young men of the 1930s and 1940s who read science fiction as kids were now creating their own new versions of these stories, and it was apocalyptic. Giant ants and strange creatures from outerspace ruled the Saturday afternoon matinee. This was the age of Elvis and Marilyn!

America in the 1950s was not quite sedate. It was a country on the move.

It was a country in Technicolor. In the photograph on page 59 of the aptly named Look Photography store, they are already advertising color Kodak film. This was not going to be a decade that was satisfied with the old ways.

Dress was becoming a little more casual, a little more rebellious. Look at the exuberant young men and women on page 61 in their leather jackets and with their slicked-back hair, cigarettes and big, wide smiles. There was nothing going to hold them back. The young women modeling on page 65 would have caused a little conversation just a few years before.

These were the days when baseball stars were becoming bigger than life. Ted Williams was the local New England hero, but there were others, like Mickey Mantle, who may have been booed but also inspired a generation of boys to put on a baseball uniform in the hope that they, too, would one day hit a home run in the World Series. Baseball was still America's sport in the 1950s, it was America's pastime. (See page 70.)

But we also see that some things do not change. Disaster can still strike without warning. Young men and women still get married. People open their own businesses hoping for success. New tools come in to replace the old.

But as picture after picture in this section also attests, as much as we looked ahead, we also always took the time to look back and celebrate where we came from and who we were.

— Lars Trodson

OPPOSITE: Lawrence Police Chief Charles F. Hart, center, stands next to a youngster decked out with his bike for the Lawrence Centennial parade in 1953.
COURTESY LAWRENCE HISTORY CENTER

RIGHT: Civil defense unit in front of the Salem Fire Department in the 1940s. These civil defense units lasted into the 1950s. COURTESY SALEM HISTORICAL SOCIETY

BOTTOM RIGHT: Wilfred Johnson, of Windham, N.H., ready to deliver milk to his Salem customers, circa 1950. COURTESY MARY T. JOHNSON

BELOW: George 'Sailor Joe' Randall at wood heel shop in Haverhill, 1950s. Randall is working on edge setting machine. COURTESY RON RANDALL

LEFT: Sacred Hearts Grammar School, class of 1950, Bradford. The Rev. Father Madden is in center and James Costello is to his left. COURTESY ELAINE C. COSTELLO

BELOW: DeMolay Boys and Rainbow Girls (affiliated with the Masons) on stage at the old Haverhill High School auditorium, circa 1950. Ralph Chapman (left) and Dave Campbell are seated at center stage. Ben Bixby is on the left with tamborine. COURTESY RON RANDALL

RIGHT: Catalano's Market at the corner of Newbury and Summer streets, Lawrence, circa, 1950. COURTESY KAY CATALANO DEBURRO

BOTTOM RIGHT: Interior of hardware store in Haverhill, circa 1950. COURTESY RON RANDALL

BELOW: View of Concord Street in Lawrence, circa 1950. COURTESY LAWRENCE HISTORY CENTER

ABOVE: Will Bragg at his photo concession inside Mitchell's Department Store in Haverhill, circa 1950. COURTESY RON RANDALL

TOP RIGHT: Interior of Mitchell's Department Store in Haverhill, circa 1950. COURTESY RON RANDALL

RIGHT: Interior of Look Photography, owned by Donald Look, Andover. COURTESY ANDOVER HISTORICAL SOCIETY

TOP: Packard School students, Lawrence, 1950. Front row, from left: George Saalfrank, Charles Andrew, Tony Lurnari, William Soper, Robert Poremba, Robert Venti, Robert Rancourt, Ray Wilson, Anthony Spitaleri. Middle row: Regis Delaney, Eleanor Leonard, Barbara Le Branc, Carmela Cali, Mr. John MacGilvrey, Joan Dyleski, Marie Meyer, Kathleen Eldred, Maire DeMauro. Back row: Jacqueline Gallant, Barbara Goodsell, Barbara Hill, Marjorie Crossman, Salvatore Branco, Arthur Desrosiers, Shirley Adams, Gloria Kennedy, Delores Berthel, Judith DeCourcey, Mary Jean Herward. Missing from the photo are Thomas Nutter and Thomas Smith. The school later became Packard Square and is owned by the firm of Lopez, Chaff and Wiesman Associates. Bill Chaff is the son of graduate Barbara Hill. COURTESY BARBARA E. HILL-CHAFF

BOTTOM: John Breen School eighth grade students, Lawrence 1950. Students are: Diane Sutcliffe, Charles Durkin, Mary Finacharo, Anthony Cestrone, Tom Bradley, Amos Poulin, Bertha Wescott, Catherine McPhee, Audrey Burke, Nina Bellia, Rose Battiato, Carol Karolunos, Diane Barker, Donald Greole, Lois Haigh, Margie Duggan (second row, second from front), Agnes Panorelli, Brendan Bresnahan, Richard Riley, Pat Caffrey, Claire Caffery, Barbara Lord. In back are Principal Higgins and teacher Miss Weinman. COURTESY MARGIE DUGGAN PATNAUDE

OPPOSITE: Haverhill High School students at a football game, circa 1950. The young man on the crutches is Freddy Burnham. Also pictured are William H. 'Billy' Ryan, left with cigarette, who would later become mayor of Haverhill, and Charlie Sterns, right of Ryan. COURTESY RON RANDALL

ABOVE: Lawrence High School class of 1930 20th reunion at the Andover Country Club in 1950. COURTESY NANCY MARCOUX

LEFT: Testimonial banquet held at Central Catholic High School auditorium for Deputy Chief Daniel P. Kiley of the Lawrence Police Department, June 18, 1950. COURTESY JOSEPH BELLA COLLECTION

RIGHT: Lawrence High School class of 1930 20th reunion planning committee in 1950. Seventh from the left in the back row is Walter J. Coleman. COURTESY NANCY MARCOUX

ABOVE: A friendly game of tug-of-war during the Hamblet employees picnic at Juniper Park in Methuen, circa 1950.
COURTESY LAWRENCE HISTORY CENTER

TOP LEFT: Participants in a girls' bicycle-decorating event at Drummond Playground, North Andover, circa 1950.
COURTESY NORTH ANDOVER HISTORICAL SOCIETY

LEFT: Gunny sack race at Drummond Playground, North Andover, circa 1950.
COURTESY NORTH ANDOVER HISTORICAL SOCIETY

ABOVE: Mario Pennisi, proud of his vegetable garden at 9 Elm Street, Lawrence, 1950.
COURTESY MAUREEN TOOHEY-CURLEY

RIGHT TOP: Irving E. Rogers, Jr., John Ahearn and Eddie Wunderlich display memorabilia for Old Gold Cigarettes at the Eagle-Tribune newspaper office.
COURTESY LAWRENCE HISTORY CENTER

RIGHT BOTTOM: St. Mark's Methodist Church Sunday School party, 1952. Children, front row from left: Barbara Bennett, Cheryl Berthel, three unidentified. Second row: Bernice Bennett, Ada Ashworth, Beatrice Crouch, Mrs. Burnham, Mrs. Robinson. Back row: Bernice Beals, Marjory Berthel, Louise Smith. Holding child at right is Beatrice Bartula. COURTESY BARBARA BARRACLOUGH

ABOVE: Dance at Punchard High School in Andover, 1950s.
COURTESY ANDOVER HISTORICAL SOCIETY

LEFT: Models from the fashion show sponsored by Tyer Rubber Co., Andover, circa 1950. COURTESY ANDOVER HISTORICAL SOCIETY

BELOW: A fashion show sponsored by Tyer Rubber Co., Andover, circa 1950. COURTESY ANDOVER HISTORICAL SOCIETY

ABOVE: North Andover Garden Club members on the grounds of the Parson Barnard House (North Andover Historical Society), Betty Harriman, Helen Hanson, Lucy Leland, Joan Hammond and Katherine Osgood. COURTESY NORTH ANDOVER HISTORICAL SOCIETY

ABOVE: Shawsheen Women's Club annual meeting in Andover, May 1950.
COURTESY ANDOVER HISTORICAL SOCIETY

RIGHT: Students attend the Pike School graduation dance in Andover, 1950. Front row: Ann Norwood, Marie Durso, Suzanne Fraser, George Benedict, Ann Plaistead, Leslie Burgiel, Barbara Emmons and Anne Howes. Back row: Gayton Osgood, Everett Scannell, John Bride, James Bride and Herald Witworth. COURTESY BARBARA INNES

ABOVE: Bus driver in Haverhill, circa 1951. COURTESY RON RANDALL

BELOW: Radio personality Forrest Neville Morgan, 1952.
COURTESY LAWRENCE HISTORY CENTER

ABOVE: Haverhill High
School classroom, circa 1951.
COURTESY RON RANDALL

LEFT: Local DJ 'Pete
Ward' in studio, 1952.
COURTESY LAWRENCE HISTORY CENTER

ABOVE: Gov. Christian A. Herter meets with Methuen Women's Republican Club in the early 1950s. In back, second from left is Dorothy Moore Giles. COURTESY SANDRA GILES PERRAULT

TOP RIGHT: A special Massachusetts Legislative Textile Commission visits Lawrence to investigate the state of the textile mills and what could be done to keep them in the city, early 1950s. Standing second from the left is Republican House Leader Frank S. Giles, of Methuen, who worked in the Arlington Mills as a young man. COURTESY SANDRA GILES PERRAULT

RIGHT: Methuen legislative delegation meets with Gov. Christian A. Herter, early 1950s. Standing, from left: Rep. Frank S. Giles, Rep. William Longworth, Rep. Thomas Slack. COURTESY SANDRA GILES PERRAULT

ABOVE: President Harry S. Truman speaking at Haverhill B & M Station, circa 1950. COURTESY RON RANDALL

BELOW: Congressman Thomas Lane, Margaret Truman and John F. Kennedy listen to a speech during a campaign stop in Lawrence, 1952. COURTESY LAWRENCE HISTORY CENTER

ABOVE: General Eisenhower comes to Lawrence to campaign for president at Lawrence Common, 1952. To his left, in front are Gov. Christian Herter and Sen. Henry Cabot Lodge. To his right in back is Massachusetts Republican House Leader Frank S. Giles. COURTESY SANDRA GILES PERRAULT

ABOVE: Punchard High School Girls Marching Band members, Andover, early 1950s.
COURTESY ANDOVER HISTORICAL SOCIETY

ABOVE: The 1951 Lawrence city champion UTWA baseball team. COURTESY LAWRENCE HISTORY CENTER

RIGHT: South Lawrence West Browns Little League baseball team, Mt. Vernon Park, Lawrence, circa 1952. Front row, from left: Robert Murphy, Charles Guido, Walter Gavribuk, Robert Bateman, Timothy Danahy, Jim Aldonis, George Kannheiser (catcher), Michael Deacy. Back row: Manager Leo Lippe, Henry Staples, Vincent Maguire, Richard Seguin, Jerry Ouellette, Richard Latulippe, Richard Fournier, Coach Dr. Raymond Ouellette.
COURTESY SANDRA KANNHEISER

TOP: Boys from the 1952 ninth grade graduating class at Central School in Methuen. The boys and girls were photographed separately because of the large size of the class.
COURTESY WALTER ANDREWS

BOTTOM: Girls from the 1952 ninth grade graduating class at Central School in Methuen.
COURTESY WALTER ANDREWS

ABOVE: Thorton's Valley Oil Co., at 15-21 White Street, Haverhill, circa 1952.
COURTESY HAVERHILL PUBLIC LIBRARY

RIGHT: First Church of the Nazarene on Winter Street, Haverhill, November 1952.
COURTESY HAVERHILL PUBLIC LIBRARY

FAR RIGHT: Community well on its way to reaching the goal for the YMCA Building Campaign in Haverhill, circa 1952.
COURTESY HAVERHILL PUBLIC LIBRARY

LEFT: Bay State Merchants National Bank Christmas party at the Red Tavern in Methuen, circa 1951. Front row, from left: Arthur Sunderland, Bertha Wessell, Ed Southwick, Mildred Batty, Ruth Goddard, Everett Merrow, Howell Stillman, Ruth Galloway, Priscilla Musk, Grace Puppularde, Eileen Proulx, Vivian Batal, Irving Hinton. Second row: Tina Pittochelli, Gert Hart, Arlene Gullar, Alan Rogers, Irene Karabashian, Bea Coleman, Bunny Kay, Rosemary Raymond, Ruth Woekel, Stella Lanory, Claire Paquette, Georgette Cross, Betty Larson, Margorie Zarwell, Sylvia Joery, Ruth Burton, Julia Vizinni, Mary Laudani, Margaret Hickey, Marilyn Golan, Lillian Pomerleau, Jimmie Vizinni. Back row: Al Mann, Fred Bean, John Richter, John Sammataru, Bill Smith, Harold Coleman, George Newall, Roy Gilbert, Fred Crosdale, Walter Mann, Andy Matchead, Harold Winter, Mike Herliky, Pete Rutter, Bill Napolitano, Russell Lord, Everett Fletcher, Willie Young. COURTESY BILL HICKEY

ABOVE: Jeannette Hayes and her children Phyllis, John and Eileen, at their home on Railroad Street, Lawrence, 1952. COURTESY EILEEN C. BURKE

LEFT: A group of youngsters pose with Santa in Methuen in 1952. COURTESY JOSEPH BELLA COLLECTION

RIGHT: The interior of George Gelt's market, located on Main Street in Salem near Route 28, circa 1953. The owner, George Gelt, was also a Salem selectman for a term. COURTESY SALEM HISTORICAL SOCIETY

OPPOSITE: Sgt. Raymond Hickey directs traffic while Charles Hillon uses the fire truck ladder over Elm Square in Andover, 1950s. COURTESY BILL DOWNS

BELOW: Grieco Brothers party, Lawrence, 1953. Pictured are Angela Scire, Nellie Balsamo and friends. COURTESY JO BALSAMO DIPAOLO

RIGHT: Gertrude Bateman teaches physical education class in the Johnson High School gym in 1953. COURTESY ELSIE POULIOT

BOTTOM RIGHT: Elaine S. Jiadosz's 1953 graduation photo from Johnson High School in North Andover. COURTESY ELAINE S. BRASSEUR

BELOW: Baseball team sponsered by Lawton's Hot Dog Stand in 1953. Lawton's was located at the corner of Broadway and Canal Street in Lawrence. Kneeling, from left: Jack Pedrick, George Bower, Ray Huot, Arthur Bower, Bob Jennings. Standing: Gillie Moran, Joe Cockroft, Henry Koza, Bob Ducheneau, Dick Croteau. COURTESY GERTRUDE CHENARD

ABOVE: The Coleman family of Lawrence, 1953. Walter and Marian with children Nancy (in Walter's arms) and Jimmy. COURTESY NANCY MARCOUX

RIGHT TOP: Donald R. Brasseur, a member of the Road Drifters Motorcycle Club, standing next to his new 1953 Indian Chief motorcycle in North Andover. COURTESY ELAINE JIADOSZ BRASSEUR

RIGHT BOTTOM: Jim and Steve Devine, Methuen, 1954. COURTESY NANCY O'NEIL

LEFT: Methuen town officials celebrate Lawrence's Centennial in 1953. From left are Selectman Elliot Vose, Rep. Frank Giles and Selectman Roger Ingalls. COURTESY SANDRA GILES PERRAULT

BOTTOM LEFT: Lawrence Centennial Parade in June of 1953. Riding on the float are Lois Leary and Claire Webber. COURTESY EAGLE-TRIBUNE ARCHIVES

OPPOSITE: Register of Deeds G. Hudson Driver and staff dressed for the 1953 Lawrence Centennial Parade, standing on the steps of the district court building on Common Street in Lawrence. Front row, from left: Peggy Hill, Evelyn Bier, Eleanore Pitocchelli, Doris Jampens and Norma McMahon. Back row: Ann Alcarese, Joan Broadhurst, Dorothy Scanlon, G. Hudson Driver, Mary Wojnar, and Peggy Wolfendale. COURTESY JOAN DUGGAN

BELOW: Holihan's float in the Lawrence Centennial Parade in June of 1953. The girl in the middle on the float is Mary Geraghty Duggan. Her husband, Jim Duggan, worked for Holihan's. COURTESY LAWRENCE HISTORY CENTER

ABOVE: Picnic at Waverly Playground, North Andover, circa 1953.
COURTESY NORTH ANDOVER HISTORICAL SOCIETY

BELOW: Decorating the roof of the shelter for Parents' Night at Waverly Playground, North Andover, circa 1953. COURTESY NORTH ANDOVER HISTORICAL SOCIETY

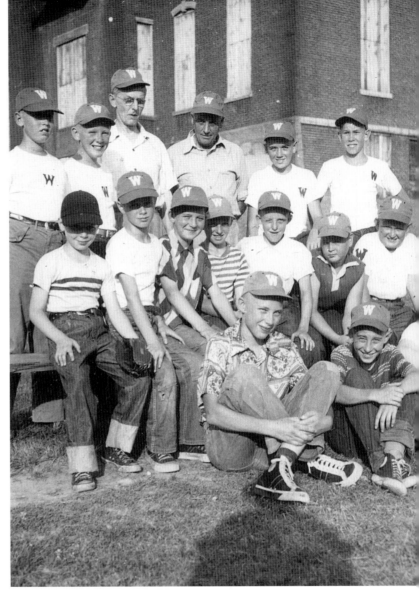

ABOVE: North Andover Community Center Baseball Team, August 1953. Front row, from left: John Wolvius, unidentified, Patrick Kilcourse. Second row: Leighton Detora, Alan Foster, unidentified, Tom McIntyre, Jack McIntyre, Benjamin Osgood, Donald Stankatis. Back row: John Chase, unidentified, Arthur Drummond, Joseph Chamberlin, Francis Chamberlin, Bruce Elliot.
COURTESY NORTH ANDOVER HISTORICAL SOCIETY

ABOVE: Costume party at Waverly Playground, North Andover, circa 1953. COURTESY NORTH ANDOVER HISTORICAL SOCIETY

LEFT: Members of North Parish Church congregation dressed for 'Heritage Sunday,' North Andover, October 1953. COURTESY NORTH ANDOVER HISTORICAL SOCIETY

ABOVE: Wilber J. Kyle, proprietor, left, helps customer Michael Murphy with his groceries at Gardella's Fruit Store, 1954. The store was at 278 Main Street in Haverhill. This photo was taken when Hurricane Carol swept through the area on August 31, 1954. COURTESY HAVERHILL PUBLIC LIBRARY

TOP RIGHT: A worker demonstrates one of the machines inside Allied Shoe Machinery bus in Haverhill, September 1954. COURTESY HAVERHILL PUBLIC LIBRARY

RIGHT: An evening sale at Elliott's, 39 Merrimack Street, Haverhill, October 1954. COURTESY HAVERHILL PUBLIC LIBRARY

ABOVE: St. Augustine's May Procession at St. Augustine's Church, Lawrence, in 1954. At far right is Jimmy Coleman. At far left is Bobby Muzerall. COURTESY NANCY MARCOUX

ABOVE: Elaine Sue Jiadosz and Donald Ralph Brasseur on their wedding day at St. Michael Church in North Andover, 1954. COURTESY ELAINE JIADOSZ BRASSEUR

LEFT: Allied Shoe Machinery bus at Washington Square, Haverhill, September 1954. This was a 'traveling' business. COURTESY HAVERHILL PUBLIC LIBRARY

ABOVE: Senior class officers of North Andover High School in 1954-55. Seated is Elsie Thomas, secretary and treasurer. Behind her from left: Charles Kettinger, vice president; Robert Kellan, president. COURTESY ELSIE POULIOT

LEFT: Methuen High School vs. Central Catholic High School basketball game at Central Catholic Auditorium, Lawrence, 1954. Going up for the shot is Scott Giles, Methuen's high point scorer three years in a row who was later inducted into the MSH Athletic Hall of Fame. Methuen's team was coached by the legendary Jack Barry. This team went to the finals of the Tech Tourney in Boston Garden. COURTESY SANDRA GILES PERRAULT

ABOVE: School friends from St. Mary's High School, Lawrence, 1954. One of the girls is from Lawrence High School. COURTESY ELEANOR PENNISI

OPPOSITE BOTTOM: The 1954 eighth grade graduating class from Alexander Bruce School, photographed at the reservoir on Tower Hill in Lawrence. The original Bruce School was destroyed by fire in March of 1951. Students grade six through eight attended the H. K. Oliver School while their school was rebuilt at its current location. Front row: Wayne Hamilton, unidentified, Sandy Poulin, Douglas Taylor, Doris Hershfield, Alan Lebowitz, Rosemary Houle, Alan LeVasseur, Michaela Rosenberg, Dick Reming, Rosemary Sarcione, J. Fleischman, Ilene Junkins, Robert Kaplan, Dorothy Watson, John Watson, John Neilon, Kathryn Cheas, Dennis LeBrecque, Linda Fiore. Second row: Francis Holmes, unidentified, B. Dillon, Rosalind Berger, James Hennessey, Phyllis Hassey, Alan Daigault, Dolores Silva, Albert Spirdione, Irene Deschamps, Stuart Soreff, Linda Taylor, Norman Theriault, two unidentified, Suzanne McHugh, James Akimchuck, Eva Lefebre. Third row: Owen Barrett, unidentified, J. Gonet, unidentified, Stephen Woloshin, Marilyn Signor, Laurence Collopy, Carolyn Baker, H. Anderson, Marilyn Signor, unidentified, Roberta Messier, Thomas Gibbons, unidentified, unidentified, unidentified, Thomas Healy, Jacqueline Bobek, Hector Turcotte, unidentified, Mary Ellen Gould, William Fire. Back row: Principal John Fleming, Mary Flathers, Elaine Orr, two unidentified, Barbara Mottram, Arlene Midore, Freya Feinman, Joanne Geraci, Cynthia Mandros, unidentified, Madeline Schuman, Norma Kibildis, Marjorie Hymanson, Joyce Peterson, James Blanchette, Gertrude Bowes, two unidentified, Eugene Ducheneau, Irene Gagne, E. Gonet, Claire Myers, two unidentified. COURTESY MARY ANN (FLATHERS) ANDREWS AND DICK REMING

BELOW: Johnson High School Junior/Senior Prom Grand March, 1954. This was the last prom at Johnson High School at Main and Osgood streets in North Andover. COURTESY ELSIE POULIOT

BOTTOM: Graduates from St. Mary's High School, Lawrence, 1954. COURTESY ELEANOR PENNISI

LEFT: Damage to the Johnson Cottage in the wake of Hurricane Carol in 1954. COURTESY NORTH ANDOVER HISTORICAL SOCIETY

BELOW: Boaters paddle through an Andover park after Hurricane Carol in 1954. COURTESY ANDOVER HISTORICAL SOCIETY

ABOVE: Aftermath of Hurricane Carol on Grand Street in Haverhill, August 1954. COURTESY RON RANDALL

OPPOSITE: High water in Andover after the 1954 hurricane swept through the area. COURTESY ANDOVER HISTORICAL SOCIETY

RIGHT: Firemen extinguish a fire on Water Street in Haverhill, December 1954.
COURTESY HAVERHILL PUBLIC LIBRARY

BOTTOM RIGHT: Two generations of Andover firefighters at the Andover Country Club for a testimonial for new Fire Chief Henry Lester Hilton in 1955. From left are Chief Henry L. Hilton, his mother Elizabeth Hilton, his wife Leona Hilton and father Lester Hilton, who retired two years earlier as deputy fire chief after 45 years on the force. COURTESY L. E. HILTON

BELOW: Lawrence police officer Christopher M. Donovan directs traffic at the intersection of Essex and Amesbury streets, looking east, circa 1955. COURTESY MICHAEL F. DONOVAN

ABOVE: Little League baseball team at Riverside Park in Haverhill, 1955. Bill McGregor is middle row, second from left; Skip Jackson is middle row, second from right; Chris Milnes is back row, center.
COURTESY NANCY MCGREGOR

TOP LEFT: 'The Park Street Gang' playing baseball in the dead of winter, Turn Hall, Park Street, Lawrence, 1955. Pictured include Joe Smith, far right, along with Bobby Gosselin, Sammy Perruchio, Dickie Rozzi, John Walolis, Jimmy Smith and Ray Gosselin. COURTESY JOSEPH K. SMITH, JR.

LEFT: Miss Janey Knightly (in the background) taught an art class at Grogan's Playground, circa 1955.
COURTESY NORTH ANDOVER HISTORICAL SOCIETY

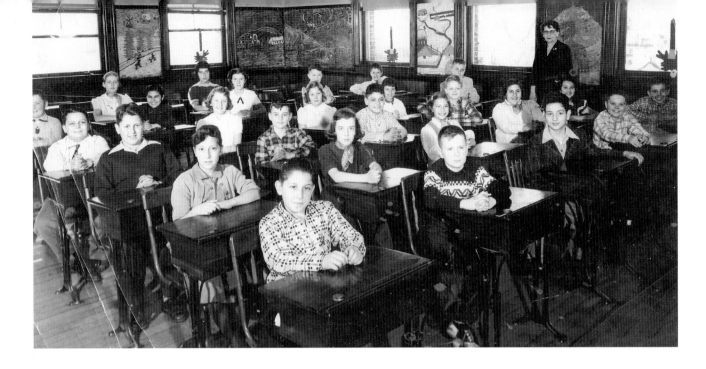

LEFT: Sixth grade students of Gilbert E. Hood School, located on Park Street in Lawrence, 1955. Bobby Marconi is front row, left; Joe Smith is front row, second from left; Anna Sullivan is the teacher. COURTESY MARIA J. SMITH

BOTTOM LEFT: Tilton School students participate in Arbor Day activities, Haverhill, 1955. COURTESY HAVERHILL PUBLIC LIBRARY

BELOW: North Andover High School Junior/Senior Prom Grand March in 1955. This was the first prom at the new North Andover High School which now serves as the North Andover Middle School. COURTESY ELSIE POULIOT

ABOVE: Paperboys picking up their loads at the corner of Willow and Park streets for evening delivery in Lawrence, 1950s. Michael Russo is one of the paperboys and Walter Johnson, the captain. COURTESY LAWRENCE HISTORY CENTER

LEFT: Students at the gates of Abbot Academy in Andover in the 1950s. COURTESY ANDOVER HISTORICAL SOCIETY

ABOVE: View of the northeast corner of Broadway and Common Street, Lawrence, circa 1955.
COURTESY LAWRENCE HISTORY CENTER

OPPOSITE: The 32nd annual Feast of the Three Saints near the corner of Common and Newbury streets in Lawrence, circa 1955. COURTESY JOSEPH BELLA COLLECTION

BELOW: Motorcycle Police Officer Ray Russus, Andover, 1950s. COURTESY ANDOVER HISTORICAL SOCIETY

ABOVE: Hec and Joe's Diner at 13 White Street, Haverhill, 1955. The new owner, Henry Enire, is at right.
COURTESY HAVERHILL PUBLIC LIBRARY

LEFT: Alan Tozier, Plaistow's only mailman in the 1950s.
COURTESY PLAISTOW HISTORICAL SOCIETY

ABOVE: Selectmen, from left are Raymond Broadhead, Arthur Kirk and William Finneran, dressed up for North Andover's Centennial Parade in 1955.
COURTESY NORTH ANDOVER HISTORICAL SOCIETY

BELOW: Participants in the North Andover Centennial parade, 1955.
COURTESY NORTH ANDOVER HISTORICAL SOCIETY

ABOVE: Reverend Ernest Brown inspects the Paul Revere & Company Bell, North Andover, 1955.
COURTESY NORTH ANDOVER HISTORICAL SOCIETY, PHOTO BY GAYTON OSGOOD

RIGHT: Centennial parade in North Andover, 1955.
COURTESY NORTH ANDOVER HISTORICAL SOCIETY

ABOVE: John McKone examines huge chain links in Methuen in 1955. The fifteen links of chain were purchased by Edward F. Searles and were placed around the Washington Monument he installed in Methuen. At the time he made the purchase he was assured the links were from the Great Chain which spanned the Hudson River during the American Revolution. Parts of the Great Chain, which was used to prevent the British forces from taking West Point in New York, were forged by Methuen resident Joshua Swan. Unfortunately, the chain Searles purchased was from a later period. He had been duped. COURTESY JOSEPH BELLA COLLECTION

LEFT: Malvina Carter cuts the cake as Father Houghton looks on during Centennial celebrations at Trinity Church in Haverhill, October 1955. COURTESY HAVERHILL PUBLIC LIBRARY

RIGHT: Knipe Bros. shoe factory, Haverhill, 1950s.
COURTESY HAVERHILL PUBLIC LIBRARY

BELOW: View at the corner of Merrimack and Emerson streets during Dollar Days in Haverhill, circa 1955.
COURTESY HAVERHILL PUBLIC LIBRARY

ABOVE: The Salem railroad depot as it looked in the 1950s. When the B&M railroad stopped running passenger service it became a law office. When vacated in 2008, it was restored by the Historical Society and is the home of the Salem Chamber of Commerce.
COURTESY SALEM HISTORICAL SOCIETY

LEFT: View of Merrimack Street, looking east, Haverhill, 1956.

BELOW: Scouts line up on the parade field in front of the Magee Lodge on the property in Raymond owned by Boy Scouts of America North Essex Council from 1929 through 2006. The camp hosted hundreds of boys from Methuen, Andover, North Andover and Lawrence. Photo circa 1956.

ABOVE: Celebration of Blessed Julie Billiart, founder of Notre Dame Sisters, at St. Mary's Church in Lawrence, 1956, before canonization in 1964. Cammy Pennisi, right, unveiled the painting by her father, Guy R. Pennisi, a well-known painter and life-long resident of Lawrence. Guy developed a love of art at a young age working with his father and brothers in the family business, the Pennisi Painting and Decorating Company. He met Antoinette Cosentino in 1933, the couple marrying three years later. Guy and Antoinette eventually started their own store, the G. R. Pennisi Company, before shutting it down in 1959 and opening the Pennisi Art Stuidio, where Guy taught over 1,000 students before closing in 1984. COURTESY ELEANOR PENNISI

LEFT: Jimmy Coleman's first communion at St. Augustine's Parish at Tower Hill in Lawrence, June 2, 1956. From left: Nancy Coleman, Michael Coleman, Jimmy Coleman. COURTESY NANCY MARCOUX

OPPOSITE: Dave, Howard, Diane and Donald Dutton in front of Piper Cub used for aerobatics in Haverhill, 1956. COURTESY DAVE DUTTON

ABOVE: Mr. and Mrs. Honore Sirois celebrating their 45th wedding anniversary in 1956 at the Lawrence Rod and Gun Club with their children Regina Laplume, 'Pete' Sirois, 'Fat' Sirois, René Sirois, 'Babe' Sirois and Isabelle Mailloux along with their grandchildren. COURTESY DONNA MAILLOUX

ABOVE: New firefighters being sworn in at Lawrence City Hall in 1956 include Charles Keenan, third from the left, and Robert J. Chamberlain, fourth from the left. COURTESY CAROL BERUBE

RIGHT: American Legion Auxiliary No. 34 of Plaistow members dressed up for a Memorial Day Parade in 1956. Front row, from left: Ora Denault, Frances Stevens, Annabel Downing, Connie Cullen, Pres., Ruth Leith, Harriet Ingalls, Thelma 'Ginger' Holmes. Second row: Marilyn Gebow, Timmy Ashford, Gigi Whiteneck, Eleanor Ingalls, Marion Brown, Mary Downing. Back row: Gladys Libby, Virginia Ingalls, Kay Fitzpatrick, Barbara Huntress. COURTESY PLAISTOW HISTORICAL SOCIETY

FAR RIGHT: Donaghue Elementary Students board the bus on the first day of school at West Shore Road, Lake Attitash, Merrimac, September 1957. COURTESY BARBARA ATKINS

ABOVE: Andover High School cheerleaders, 1958. Pat Golden, captain, is pictured in front row, center, light colored sweater. COURTESY ANDOVER HISTORICAL SOCIETY

TOP LEFT: St. Augustine's, Lawrence, Cub Scout troop, 1956. Included in the photo are Jimmy Coleman, Mark Collins, Jimmy Winn and Michael Guthrie. COURTESY NANCY MARCOUX

LEFT: Checker players at Drummond Playground, North Andover, circa 1956. Among those pictured are Joe L., Tommy Cutter, Douglas Mann and Francis Chamberlin. COURTESY NORTH ANDOVER HISTORICAL SOCIETY

BELOW: Girl Scout Brownie group, Plaistow, circa 1957. From left: Susanne Morton, Stephanie Page, Cheryl Matson, Roberta Sorenson, Cynthia Rowell, Sandra Howard, Mary Jane Jackman, Stepheny Porter, Anna Tozier, Christine LaBranche, Pamela Kimball. COURTESY PLAISTOW HISTORICAL SOCIETY

ABOVE: Lawrence High School Varsity Football Team, 1957-58, Eastern Massachusetts Class A Champions.
COURTESY LINDA TAYLOR ARVANITIS

ABOVE: St. Andrew's Church boys basketball team, Methuen, 1958. Front row, from left: Bob Thesse, Jim Hoegen, Jr., John Howard, Albert Fielding, Bob Hillis, Bob Perrault. Back row: unidentified, Reid Miller, Dave O'Brien, Rev. George Argyle, Ron Martin, Walter Fielding, Bob Chase, Jim Hoegen, Sr. COURTESY GINNY PALMIERI

LEFT: Four generations: great-grandfather Horace 'Mitt' Moore, grandmother Dorothy Moore Giles, father Scott L. Giles, baby Beth Giles. Photo taken in Methuen, October 1957.
COURTESY SANDRA GILES PERRAULT

ABOVE: People crowd the floor at the Wiers Beach Ballroom in 1957 to dance to the sounds of Tony Brown's Orchestra from Lawrence. The ballroom was dramatically lighted by several sparkling chandeliers.
COURTESY LISA (BARONE) BERNARD

TOP LEFT: Punchard High School cheerleaders, Andover. Pat Golden, captain, is pictured kneeling down in front wearing a white jumper.
COURTESY ANDOVER HISTORICAL SOCIETY

LEFT: Crowd cheers for a football game at Punchard High School in Andover, 1950s.
COURTESY ANDOVER HISTORICAL SOCIETY

ABOVE: Graduate Cammy Pennisi showing her diploma to Sister while her brother Maurice looks on, 1957. Cammy was graduating from St. Mary's High School in Lawrence. COURTESY MAUREEN TOOHEY-CURLEY

RIGHT TOP: George Washington statue being dismantled, Lawrence Street in Methuen, 1958. In the distance St. Monica's School is under construction. This is the current site of St. Monica's Church, school and convent. COURTESY STEVE MADDEN

RIGHT BOTTOM: May Queen and attendants, St. Patrick's Church, Lawrence, circa 1958. Front row, from left: Richard Lombardo, Richard Young. Second row: William Gilmore, Daniel Allen, Elizabeth Curran, (Queen) Patricia Fenton, Evelyn Lafond, Thomas Verville, Ronald Verville. Back row: James Aldonis, James Parrah, John Murphy, Paul Drouin, George Kannheiser, Thomas Purcell, Thomas Currant, Richard Quirinale. COURTESY SANDRA KANNHEISER

LEFT: Lawrence High School band under the direction of Band Master Oswald W. Vogel, 1958. Vogel was a veteran of World War II who enlisted at the age of 35. COURTESY LINDA TAYLOR ARVANITIS

BOTTOM LEFT: Lithuanian Women Club officers at Lithuanian Citizen's Club, 42 Berkeley Street, Lawrence 1958. Front row, from left: E. Petkevich, U. Penkus, A. Veckys, A. Vaitkunas. Back row: A. Shupetris, M. Legunas, Matilda Stundzia, A. Vil-lickas. COURTESY JONAS STUNDZIA

ABOVE: Michael J. Hayes on the occasion of his retirement as a janitor and head of maintenance at Washington Street School, Lawrence, 1958. The gentleman with him is Walter Witkas. COURTESY EILEEN HAYES

RIGHT: Mrs. James I. Meehan (behind podium) being inducted as president of the Lady Elks in 1958. Outgoing president Shirley Callahan stands at right. COURTESY DAVID MEEHAN

BOTTOM RIGHT: Andover Fire Chief Henry Lester Hilton leading firemen in a Memorial Day parade in downtown Andover, circa 1959. COURTESY L. E. HILTON

BELOW: Albert and Mabel Davis behind the counter of the A&P store on Elm Street in Plaistow, 1958. The young lady in front is Donna Gilman. COURTESY PLAISTOW HISTORICAL SOCIETY

ABOVE: South Lawrence Flooring Co. at 140 Easton Street, Lawrence, 1959. Lucien Joncas was the proprietor and founder of the family-owned business. The family still operates the business today under the name A & B Flooring. From left: Joe Marisola, Joe Boyd, Joe Bottai, Ron Jean, Frank Houle, Francis Ellis, Jean Rancourt, Ray Guillemette, Jack Smith, unidentified, Joe Goings, Leo Gallipeau, Emil Daignault, Henry Houle, Arthur Joncas, Lucien Joncas. COURTESY ROBERT A. JONCAS

LEFT: Ron Randall, left, and Kevin Ryan in their new Volkswagons, Haverhill, July 4, 1959. COURTESY RON RANDALL

CHAPTER THREE

THE 1960s

THIS WAS THE ERA OF "MAD MEN," ALTHOUGH THE SLICKNESS of Madison Avenue took a little more time making it to the Merrimack Valley. It was also to be another decade split in two, only unlike the 1940s, the quieter half came first.

Suburban sprawl was in bloom because these were the last years of the post-war baby boom of 1946 -1964. People were fleeing the city, and main streets across New England were trying a different approach to keep their customers.

This was the beginning of a new political era, as well. This was Massachusetts, after all, and in the first year of the decade, a man from Boston was elected president of the United States. He was a young, good looking man, this John F. Kennedy, and he too promised a new era, an era of young men who had been "tempered by war" but who were still young enough to lead. And the president had two young brothers who could be seen around the state (page 116).

Indeed, on page 117, there's a business called The Moderne Shoppe — a mixture of the old and new.

This was the decade in which the young men who had read science fiction in the 1940s and wrote it in the 1950s were able to see some of the fantastic predictions begin to come to life. Men (and monkeys) were being launched into space in the 1960s, and the space race was on.

By 1965, everyone was feeling a little freer. The women on page 126 at the White Rose Laundry company party in Methuen are showing signs of sartorial emancipation. The young man waiting for the bus in Haverhill on page 131 has adopted a mod form of dress favored by the Beatles and other groups of the era.

This was also the decade in which men and women stopped wearing hats — the men taking their cue from JFK. Outside of a fireman or a police officer, you will not find, in the photos from this decade, women wearing the latest millinery fashions or men wearing fedoras. No more silk top hats. Jackets and ties were still worn to the office, but the hat — that was so 1959.

— Lars Trodson

OPPOSITE: Lawrence Police Lt. Frank Incropera with crossing guard and school safety patrol, May 1966. COURTESY FRANCIS INCROPERA

ABOVE: Wilfred Johnson weighing corn produced on his Highland View Farm, Windham, circa 1960. COURTESY MARY T. JOHNSON

RIGHT TOP: Cities Service station at 224 South Broadway Street, Lawrence. Owners Jerry and Kay Guilmette with their employee Norman (Butch) Berube. COURTESY THE GUILMETTE FAMILY

RIGHT BOTTOM: St. Mark's Methodist Church confirmation class, 1960. Front row, from left: Donna Dainouski, unidentified, Susan Nelson. Second row: Cheryl Berthel, Barbara Bennett. Back: Rev. Homer Warfield. The church was at the corner of Essex and Margin streets in Lawrence. COURTESY BARBARA BARRACLOUGH

ABOVE: Unveiling of painting of Robert Frost and dedication of Frost School, Lawrence, 1960. The oil painting was by Guy R. Pennisi of Lawrence. COURTESY ELEANOR PENNISI

BELOW: Andover Police Chief George Ilano speaks to a youngster at police headquarters, circa 1960. COURTESY ANDOVER HISTORICAL SOCIETY

ABOVE: Youthful shoppers enjoy Lawrence Days at Grant's Department Store, circa 1960. COURTESY LAWRENCE HISTORY CENTER

BELOW: Lt. Francis Incropera, Sr. lectures two young men on the dangers of riding double, 1960. COURTESY LAWRENCE HISTORY CENTER

ABOVE: View of Elm Street, looking east toward White Street, Lawrence, circa 1960. COURTESY LAWRENCE HISTORY CENTER

BELOW: Aerial view of downtown Haverhill, circa 1961.
COURTESY HAVERHILL PUBLIC LIBRARY

ABOVE: Businesses in the 400 block of Essex Street in Lawrence included Macartney's Men's Clothing, Commercial Chambers, Community Opticians, Nugent's Women's Clothing and Korbey's, circa 1960.
COURTESY LAWRENCE HISTORY CENTER

OPPOSITE: The house at 68 Main Street, Andover, being moved to make room for Bay State Merchants Bank. The house, a three-story duplex, is located on Phillips Hill. The A&P Super Market is seen at right.
COURTESY ANDOVER HISTORICAL SOCIETY

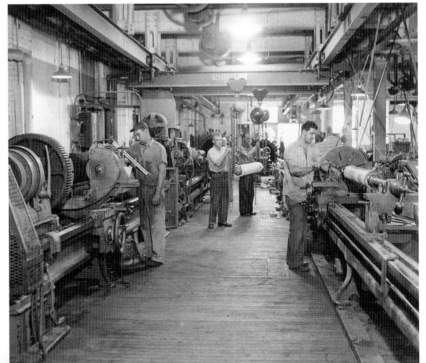

ABOVE: Bernard Goffstein and Fred Malcolm inside the vault at Haverhill Savings Bank, circa 1960. COURTESY HAVERHILL PUBLIC LIBRARY

RIGHT TOP: Gov. John A. Volpe swears in Frank S. Giles of Methuen as Massachusetts Commissioner of Public Safety while Lawrence Mayor John Buckley looks on. Mr. Giles represented Greater Lawrence in the Massachusetts House of Representatives from 1948 to 1960, becoming leader of the Republican Party. As commissioner, Mr. Giles, who began as a Methuen policeman, became head of the Massachusetts State Police. Photo taken in 1961. COURTESY SANDRA GILES PERRAULT

RIGHT BOTTOM: Tyer Rubber Co. factory, Andover. COURTESY ANDOVER HISTORICAL SOCIETY

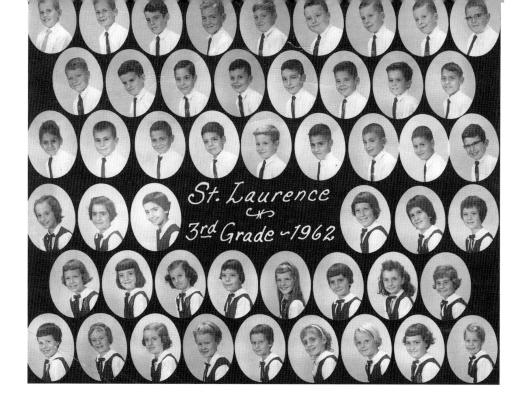

ABOVE: Story Hour at Stevens Memorial Library in North Andover, circa 1961. COURTESY NORTH ANDOVER HISTORICAL SOCIETY

TOP LEFT: St. Laurence O'Toole School, third-grade students, Lawrence, 1962. Mrs. Patricia (Carey) Quintal was the teacher. COURTESY PATRICIA QUINTAL

LEFT: Katie Rowell watches her hit sail for a home run at Landman's Field in Plaistow during the Mother and Son Game in August 1960. COURTESY PLAISTOW HISTORICAL SOCIETY

ABOVE: St. Augustine Grammar School graduation, Lawrence, 1962. Among those pictured are Marguerite Scuito, Phyllis Hayes, Pamela Dowling, Jane Donovan, Fr. Paul Judson and Rayma Kinsella. COURTESY EILEEN HAYES

RIGHT: Members of Loyalty Committee from St. Mark's Methodist Church at the corner of Essex and Margin streets, Lawrence, October 1962. The Rev. Conrad Putzig is seen shaking hands with Thomas Palmer as Bernice Bennett, Fred Bennett, Jr. (chairman), Nettie Hartwig, Bernice Beals and Ruth Palmer look on. COURTESY BARBARA BARRACLOUGH

ABOVE: Bread and Roses Parade at the corner of Green Street and Broadway in Lawrence 1962. On the float are the Spiggot Falls Hay Shakers: long-time Methuen Town Clerk Vernon Sanborn and friends. They entertained fans with corny old-time music, skits and jokes. COURTESY WILLIAM H. CHAFF, JR.

BELOW: While running for senator, Ted Kennedy attends the Western Electric Convention in North Andover, 1962. He is escorted by Western Electric engineers. COURTESY BARBARA INNES

ABOVE: Lawrence residents enjoying summertime at Seabrook Beach in 1962. Lawrence police officer Christopher M. Donovan and sons Christopher, center, and Michael at a beach cottage after a half day of mackerel fishing with Eastman's. COURTESY MICHAEL F. DONOVAN

LEFT TOP: The Moderne Shoppe on Route 110 in Methuen, circa 1962. COURTESY ADDIE CARUSO

LEFT BOTTOM: A reception honoring Mayor Buckley was held at Freedman's Hall in 1962. On Buckley's left is Lawrence native and Broadway star Robert Goulet. COURTESY LAWRENCE HISTORY CENTER

ABOVE: A view of Washington Square, looking east from Washington Street, Haverhill, 1960s. COURTESY HAVERHILL PUBLIC LIBRARY

TOP RIGHT: First Baptist Church on Main Street, Haverhill, October 1962. COURTESY HAVERHILL PUBLIC LIBRARY

RIGHT: Patrons line up to attend a concert on November 3, 1963 at Methuen Memorial Music Hall on Broadway. The concert was held to celebrate the 100th anniversary of 'The Great Organ.' COURTESY ED SAMPSON

ABOVE: Students from St. Mary's Parish march in the God and Country parade in Lawrence, 1962.
COURTESY LAWRENCE PUBLIC LIBRARY

LEFT: God and Country Parade goes by the Eagle-Tribune building in Lawrence, 1962.
COURTESY LAWRENCE PUBLIC LIBRARY

BELOW: God and Country parade in Lawrence, 1962. COURTESY LAWRENCE PUBLIC LIBRARY

ABOVE: Ted Kennedy participates in a parade in Lawrence in 1962.
COURTESY LAWRENCE HISTORY CENTER

OPPOSITE: Young children wave their flags during the God and Country parade in Lawrence, 1962. COURTESY LAWRENCE PUBLIC LIBRARY

ABOVE: New England Telephone and Telegraph Company float in a 1962 parade in Lawrence.
COURTESY LAWRENCE HISTORY CENTER

RIGHT: Davis & Furber Textile Machinery entry in the God and Country Parade in Lawrence, 1962.
COURTESY LAWRENCE PUBLIC LIBRARY

ABOVE: Relaxing with Lawrence's own Holihan's beer in Methuen, circa 1964. Seated, from left: Catherine Duggan, Anna Myers, Emma Devine. Standing: Bernie Elston, two unidentified, Jimmy Duggan, Chris Devine, Clary Myers. COURTESY NANCY O'NEIL

BELOW: Lawrence Alderman of Health and Charities Jerry Guilmette's 1964 holiday greeting card. It was an annual tradition for city politicians to send seasonal greeting cards. COURTESY THE GUILMETTE FAMILY

Merry Christmas   Happy New Year

"The Jerry Guilmettes," 1964

ABOVE: Dignitaries at Lithuanian Citizen's Club, 41 Berkeley Street in Lawrence, February 16, 1963. After Vatican II, the first celebration of Lithuanian Independence Day, when the Roman Catholic priest celebrated with the National Catholic Priest. From left are state Sen. William X. Wall, Rev. Juras, Mayor Buckley, John Stundza (club president), Rev. Gasarunas and John Urbonas. COURTESY JONAS STUNDZIA

TOP: Five generations of the Innes family: Jessie Russell, Kevin Innes, Thelma Muller, Robert Innes, Jr., Julius Kryda, Robert Innes and Duane Innes in Andover, 1963. COURTESY BARBARA INNES

LEFT: Joseph J. 'Bob' Lambert, owner of Modeler's Haven on Manchester Street in Lawrence, started the business out of his home on Tower Hill before moving to stores on Park and Hampshire streets and then Manchester Street. Photo circa 1965. COURTESY CAROL BERUBE

BOTTOM LEFT: Posternak's Kosher Market at 286 Lowell Street in Lawrence in the 1960s. The man in the center is Joe Posternak. At right is Andy Feinman. Joe's father is at left. COURTESY JOSEPH BELLA COLLECTION

BELOW: Mary E. Walsh and Francis E. Walsh behind the counter of Walsh's General Store in Plaistow in the 1960s. COURTESY PLAISTOW HISTORICAL SOCIETY

St. Laurence
1st Grade - 1963

TOP: Sister Michelle's sixth-grade class at St. Augustine's School on Tower Hill in Lawrence, circa 1963. Rows listed right to left, names listed front to back. First Row: Linda Saracusa, John Holtham, Donna Bourassa. Second Row: Donna Donohue, Kenneth Bourassa, Linda Diorio, Bill Lannon, Jean Toher, Thomas Guthrie, Barbara McGuire, John Webb, Judith Sullivan. Third Row: Peter Boyle, Susan Fay, Michael Connelly, Donna Garfi, Dennis McGuire, Mareen Gearin, Peter Dowling, Beverly Poirier, David Meehan, Denise Bretton. Fourth Row: Robert Godin, Debbie Griffin, Michael Beauchamp, Maureen Holt, Gail Jackson, Margaret Mimno, Dennis Dyer, Lorraine Voyeur, Richard Bernardin. Fifth Row: John Golden, Paula May Calderone, John Sullivan, Mareen Hewett, Michael Therrien, Carol Khory, Kevin Craddock, Jacqueline Bouvier. Sixth Row: Neil Carney, Pauline Guy, Paul Griffin, Beverly Fallon, Stephen Letendre, Patricia Holland, Paul Rivet. Back Row: Dennis Guilmette, Mary Lou Traynor, Paul Blouin, Mary Lou Rottler, Daniel Foley, Mary Abate, Joanne Webb, Richard LeFleur, Mary Beth Fitzgerald, Patrica O'Claire, Edward Gaffney, Joseph Baggett, Sister Michelle (Teacher). COURTESY DAVID MEEHAN

BOTTOM: Teacher Mary Beaumont (rear left) with student teacher Jane Hanlon and their 1963-1964 class at Ashford School in Methuen. Students: Martha Ford, Joanne McCormick, Joelle Heffner, William Lane, Paula Morin, Sharon Cloutier, William Enman, Paula Zarzour, David Kirsch, Doreen Piazza, Steven Roddy, Deborah Klier, Stephanie Simpson, Arthur Krikorian, David Harb, Marilyn Jarosz, Patricia Ryan, Paula Baker, Philip Antone, Joseph Nicolosi, Frances Maniscalo, Kathryn Federico, Charles Takesian, Marie Sarto, Albert Denuzzio, Ann Marie Pizzano, Charles Messina, Harold Kazanjian. COURTESY CHARLES TAKESIAN

OPPOSITE: St. Laurence O'Toole Grammar School, first-grade class of 1963. The school was located on the corner of Newbury and East Haverhill streets in Lawrence. Top row, from left: Martin Clement, Thomas Quintel, two unidentified, Peter Blanchette, Phillip McGowan, Shane Martin, Charles Brooks, Robert O'Donald, unidentified. Second row: Bernard Smith, Phillip Dussault, unidentified, James Dawaliby, Timothy Divaney, Thaddius Paulack, Paul Laudani, unidentified, Timothy Casey, Steven Marincelli. Third row: Leila Martone, Claire Parrino, Susan Barry, Donna Robillard, Bonita Hajjar, unidentified. Fourth row: Louise Bodenrader, Elena Lucchesi, Laura Consentino, Mary Jane McKenna, Kathleen Hussey, Diane Pare, Patricia Hickel, Linda Dadducci, Linda Rogers. Fifth row: Anne Marie Perricho, Donna Constantineau, Joan Hart, Nancy Kasheta, unidentified, Laurie Albach, Judith Morrison, Ellen Quintel, Karen Lynch. Bottom row: unidentified, Doreen Hajjar, Maureen Thomas, Caryn Caraldi, Mary Bresnahan, Mary Scionte, Karen Connors, unidentified, Maureen Murphy. COURTESY LINDA DADDUCCI BOLIS

ABOVE: White Rose Laundry employee Christmas party, the year they merged with Anton's Cleaners, 1965. The party was at the Spear house in Lowell. White Rose Laundry was located on Jackson Street in Methuen. Among those pictured are Josie Caruso, Rose DiPrima, Brenda DiPrima, Marcia DiPrima, John Anton, Rose Palermo, Josie Dadducci, Claire Bistany, Dot Norcia, Carman Barbagallo, Frank Barbagallo, Sox Anton, Arthur Anton, Joe Caruso, Dominic DiPrima, Angelo Marino, John Brown and Alex Anton. COURTESY JOSIE FERRARA DADDUCCI

BELOW: View of Mechanics Blocks, fronting on Orchard Street (built before 1853), Lawrence. Photo, circa 1965. COURTESY LAWRENCE HISTORY CENTER

ABOVE: Lawrence Redevelopment Authority giving a check to homeowners who had to relocate from the Plains area in the 1960s. Top Row, from left: Rene LaCharitie, LRA Director Thomas Walsh and former LRA Director John Sirois. COURTESY LAWRENCE HISTORY CENTER

TOP: St. Monica School Brownie Troop 101 at the first tree planting on the grounds of the newly constructed Methuen Town Hall on Hampshire Street, April 1964. Front row, from left: Cheryl Walsh, Barbara Blinn, Kathleen Hill, Marilyn Foster, Maureen Burke, Robin Hill, Lee Ann Graham, Lisa Moses. Second row: Troop leaders Mrs. Dorothea Burke & Mrs. Mona Hill. The Methuen City Hall is now located on Pleasant Street. The former Town Hall was renamed the Quinn Public Safety Building. COURTESY MAUREEN BURKE

TOP: Methuen Auxiliary Police, 25 years of service, 1966. From left: Augustine Keleher, Gustave Hering, Thomas Leone, Gov. John Volpe, Clarence Chaff, Alwyn Russell, Norbert Faul. COURTESY GINNY PALMIERI

BOTTOM: Lawrence police force with Alderman Vincent Foley and Chief Charles Hart in front of the police station in Lawrence in 1965. Frank Incropera is front row, second from right. COURTESY FRANCIS INCROPERA

RIGHT TOP: Group gathers at Lawrence Democratic Headquarters at the corner of Hampshire and Essex streets, 1966. From left: Assistant Attorney General George W. Arvanitis, Auditor Ted Buczko, Lt. Governor candidate Joseph E. McGuire, Attorney General candidate Francis X. Bellotti, Alderman James O'Neil, Lawrence Democratic Committee chairperson Virginia Brady, Representative Larry Smith, Senate candidate Chub Peabody, Young Democrats of Greater Lawrence president J. Kenneth Taylor, Rep. John Bresnahan, unidentified. COURTESY LINDA TAYLOR ARVANITIS

RIGHT BOTTOM: Marian and Joe Sullivan, members of Turkey Town Trotters, North Andover, 1965. COURTESY NORTH ANDOVER HISTORICAL SOCIETY

BELOW: Turkey Town Trotters of North Andover, 1965. Shown are Jack Scanlon, Louis Tartaglione, Fran Graham, Harold Cleary and Marjorie Hunter. COURTESY NORTH ANDOVER HISTORICAL SOCIETY

ABOVE: St. Monica School first graduating class, June 12, 1966. Front row, from left: Scott McGurn, John Lavery, Monica Abdallah, Patricia Cain, Roseanne Consentino, Nancy DiSalvo, Marilyn Tardugno, Cynthia Ruggerio, Sr. Helen Julia S.N.D. (Principal), Monsignor John F. Broderick (pastor), Deborah DiSalvo, Sharon Burns, Rosemary Nolan, Karen DeLucia, David Lee, John Bradley. Second Row: Sr. Marie Roberts S.N.D., Pamela Mallen, Therese Helbick, Jean Kenney, Patricia Ward, Sheila Burdin, Michelle Arsenault, Christine Pepin, Elizabeth Burns, Kathleen Hill, Debra Fillipon, Patricia Palermo, Robert Burdin, James Graham, Robert Lavoie, John Mesrobian, Charles Marsden, Edward Brindle, Peter Carrozza, Raymond English, Bruce O'Connell, Neil Kelley, Kenneth Szostak, Thomas Sabbagh, Sr. Theresa St. Joseph, S.N.D. Third row: John Perillo, Phillip Marcello, Richard Russell, Gregory Perry, Robert Jackson, John L'Italien, Richard Hillard, Brian Parent, Augustine Fiore, Frederick Koerner, Brenda Korbey, Valerie Kirkman, Diane Bonaccorsi, Deborah Fay, Carolyn Marcello, Marilyn Foster, Elaine Autieri, Joyce Coco, Janice Sullivan. Fourth row: Brian Manning, Daniel Bulmer, Deborah Ebert, Mary Chernosky, Deborah Connors, Maureen Burke, Lynne Carter, Barbara Blinn, Denise Quarterone, Debra Arraj, Kathleen Ellis, Carol Lavoie, Joan Concanon, Patricia Scannell, Ronald Bergeron, Paul Frechette. Fifth row: William McKay, Pedro Jimenez, David Salach, Francis Michalewicz, Howard Camuso, Frances Laratonda, Thomas Masoud. Missing from photo: Stephen Devine. COURTESY MAUREEN BURKE

LEFT: St. Patrick's Grammar School 1967 graduating class of 105 students. Baby boomers flooded the public and parochial schools systems in the 1950s and 1960s. This very large graduating class is indicative of that era. Third row at far left is Rt. Rev. Monsignor Joseph P. Burke, pastor of St. Patrick's Church and a leading religious figure in the city of Lawrence for many years. Third row at far right is Father Kelly, a popular St. Patrick's Parish priest. COURTESY MICHAEL F. DONOVAN

ABOVE: Jacques Bros. Barber Shop at 234 Broadway in Lawrence, circa 1966. Brothers and proprietors Alcide G. Jacques, standing left, and Gedeon 'Gene' Jacques, standing second from left, operated the business from the early 1930s to the mid-1970s. COURTESY RUSSELL K. JACQUES

RIGHT: Ribbon-cutting ceremony at W.T. Grant Store at Westgate Shopping Center in Haverhill, November 3, 1966. From left are, Mrs. Willard O'Brien, George E. McGregor, pres. Haverhill National Bank; Herbert B. Mershon, City Councilor George K. Kartaros, Health Superintendent John J. Murphy, Edward Celtin, Herbert Brassuer, Mayor Paul Chase, Richard C. Trumble, City Manager Walter E. Lawrence, City Councilor Edward M. Nordengren, Gazette Publisher Raymond V. McNamara, Arthur S. Lehne, City Councilor David M. Baker, John P. Dane and Mrs. Marilyn E. Berman. COURTESY HAVERHILL PUBLIC LIBRARY

LEFT: This Methuen diner located next to the Odd Fellows building on Hampshire Street was known as Brown's or Brownies in the 1940s and 1950s. In the late 1950s the name was changed to Linda's Diner, which had a relatively short life in Methuen history. The diner was eventually razed and a parking lot was created on the site. COURTESY JOSEPH BELLA COLLECTION

BOTTOM LEFT: View of Merrimack Street, Haverhill, 1968. This gentleman is waiting for the bus under heat lamp at Haverhill Gas Co. COURTESY HAVERHILL PUBLIC LIBRARY

ABOVE: The Coleman family at the Eagle-Tribune's dedication of its new building in North Andover in 1968. From left: Nancy, Marian, Walter J. (employee of the newspaper), Jimmy and Michael Coleman. COURTESY NANCY MARCOUX

TOP: St. Laurence O'Toole Grammar School Glee Club under the direction of Sr. Rose Vincent, S.N.D. This photo was taken at Parish Hall in Lawrence, December 19, 1968. The hall was located on the corner of Newbury and East Haverhill streets. Girls from grades 5-8 participated in the annual Christmas Concert. Glee club members include: Laurie Albach, Jayne Aufiero, Susan Barry, Linda Berry, Louise Bodenrader, Patricia Bresnahan, Caryn Caraldi, Ann Casey, Karen Connors, Teresa Consentino, Donna Constantineau, Kim Crompton, Nancy Cunningham, Linda Jean Dadducci, Marie DiDio, Maureen Dooley, Elizabeth Dwindells, Veronica Dwindells, Nadine Facela, Sharon Finnigan, Paula Garvis, Annee Marie Girouard, Doreen Hajjar, Nancy Kasheta, Elena Lucchesi, Felicia Maccarone, Marie Malori, Lelia Martone, Mary Jane McKenna, Judy Morrison, Colleen Neel, Mary Ellen O'Donnell, Linda O'Neil, Claire Parrino, Karen Picone, Linda Rogers, Mary-Jo Ruel, Barbara Seed, Mary Scionte, Anne Mary Sheehy, Rosemary Sullivan, Maureen Thomas, Christine Traynor and Eileen Wills.
COURTESY LINDA DADDUCCI BOLIS

BOTTOM: Sisters Marie Charles, Mary Rose, Julie Peter, Ellen Elizabeth, Rose Vincent and Sean Marguerite, have their photo taken with Collette Donahue and Theresa Clement. These sisters were from Saint Agatha Convent in Milton, 1968.
COURTESY LAWRENCE HISTORY CENTER

ABOVE: View of Merrimack Street, Haverhill, 1968. COURTESY HAVERHILL PUBLIC LIBRARY

TOP LEFT: McQuade Library on the campus of Merrimack College, circa 1967. COURTESY NORTH ANDOVER HISTORICAL SOCIETY

LEFT: Aerial view of Dutton Airport and Kenoza Lake off Route 108, Haverhill, circa 1969. COURTESY DAVE DUTTON

LEFT: East Junior High School, ninth grade class, June 1969. COURTESY ANDOVER HISTORICAL SOCIETY

FAR LEFT: John F. Hayes, Lawrence Fire Department, when he was named Deputy Fire Chief in 1969. COURTESY EILEEN HAYES

BELOW: View of Main Street from Elm Square, Andover, circa 1969. COURTESY ANDOVER HISTORICAL SOCIETY

ABOVE: World War I Veterans, Members of Battery F., 102nd Field Artillery, 26th Yankee Division, celebrating Golden Anniversary of Discharge in 1919 at Rolling Green, May 24, 1969. Front row, from left: William H. Cronshaw, Charles Bowman, Edward J. Desaulnier, Richard F. Hadley, Theodore R. Johnson, Alfred Laliberte, Charles Defazio, Armand J. Lepine, Carlton R. Hosley, Martin Gilligan. Second row: George H. Johnson, Philip J. White, James H. Buss, John King, Walter P. Mitchell, Albert G. Sparks, Minton A. Winslow, George C. Napier, Arthur Cole, Bryan Leonard. Back row: Brackett Parsons, John M. Erving, Eldred Larkin, Raymond F. Corkery. COURTESY ANDOVER HISTORICAL SOCIETY

BUSINESS PROFILES

The businesses and community leaders profiled on the pages that follow have made countless important contributions to the vitality of the Merrimack Valley over many years, and they continue to do so today. The Eagle-Tribune wishes to thank these organizations and individuals for their contributions to our community and to this historical celebration.

A special thank you is extended to Northern Essex Community College for its generous support, and for all of it has done to make our community stronger, healthier and more vibrant.

ABOVE: Northern Essex Community College's rural 106-acre campus in Haverhill includes the David Hartleb Technology Center and the Harold Bentley Library.

For the past 50 years, Northern Essex Community College has been privileged to be a part of the extraordinary Merrimack Valley Community. We are proud of the contributions we have made—we have educated thousands of students over the years, providing them with the academic credentials to succeed in life.

This beautiful book captures the spirit of our community by featuring the people, events, and institutions that played an important role in shaping who we are today.

We salute our community partners and look forward to continuing to make history in the Merrimack Valley.

Northern Essex
Community College

HAVERHILL • LAWRENCE

NORTHERN ESSEX COMMUNITY COLLEGE

Since 1961

Northern Essex Community College opened its doors at the former Greenleaf Elementary School in Bradford 50 years ago. There were 186 students that first year. Most were recent high school graduates who planned to get a liberal arts degree and transfer to a four-year college. At that time, there were just five majors to choose from: Liberal Arts Transfer, General Studies, Business Administration, Secretarial, and Electronic Technology.

Today, Northern Essex has a 106-acre suburban campus in Haverhill; a rapidly expanding urban campus in downtown Lawrence; and programs, services, and partnerships across the Merrimack Valley. Over 7,400 credit students study days, evenings, weekends, and online, and an additional 6,700 take noncredit workforce development and community education courses.

The college now offers over 90 certificate and associate degree programs in fields such as health care, criminal justice, and technology. While most Northern Essex students plan to transfer after Northern Essex to four-year colleges and universities, many are enrolled in career programs designed to prepare them for immediate placement in jobs after graduation. The college works closely with area employers to create programs in high demand areas. Recent examples include associate degrees in lab science and paramedic technology and certificates in computer forensics and sleep technology.

Northern Essex prides itself on its quality programs, its flexible scheduling, and its focus on student success. Many highly successful individuals got their start at Northern Essex including Tom Bergeron, television personality; Lou Schwechheimer, vice president and general manager of the Pawtucket Red Sox; Phil Starks, biology professor, Tufts University; Dan Lyons, technology columnist, Newsweek Magazine; and Steve Bedrosian, former major league baseball player and winner of the Cy Young Award.

Northern Essex Community College

100 Elliott St., Haverhill, MA 01830 • 45 Franklin St., Lawrence, MA 01842 • www.necc.mass.edu

Northern Essex's John R. Dimitry Building in Lawrence was donated to the Commonwealth by the Prudential Insurance Company in 1991.

Located near Kenoza Lake, Northern Essex's beautifully landscaped, 106-acre Haverhill Campus features eight buildings including the David Hartleb Technology Center and the award winning Behrakis One Stop Student Center.

MINCO DEVELOPMENT CORPORATION

Since 1937

ITS HERITAGE FOUNDED IN GREATER LAWRENCE 75 YEARS AGO

In 1937, Louis P. Minicucci, Sr. had a vision to begin a diversified portfolio of business ventures, laying the foundation for the modern day enterprise known as Minco Development Corporation.

At the age of 18, he operated a service station, which eventually led to the creation of the Minicucci Oil Company. A wholesale and retail home heating oil distribution business, it maintained a sizeable plant storage facility in Methuen. At the height of this prosperous business, Lou, Sr. enlisted in the U.S. Army during World War II and was assigned to the 45th Infantry Division Anti-Tank Company under General George S. Patton. Fighting in the front lines for over 511 days, he earned the Infantry Combat Metal and the Bronze Star.

Upon returning from the war, he invested in Dairy Queen and purchased the trade name, creating Dairy Queen of Boston, Inc., which operates to this day in Suffolk, Essex and Middlesex Counties. It is one of the oldest continuous territory operators in the U.S., dating back 60 years.

In 1982, his son, Louis P. Minicucci, Jr., an MBA and Harvard University alumnus, incorporated Minco Development Corporation, a full service commercial real estate company, which has developed over 1,500 units of residential housing, the Methuen CVS and the North Andover Stop & Shop, to name a few local projects. Minco has also developed properties or invested in real estate through various entities in Florida, Arizona, Rhode Island, Maine, Connecticut and New Hampshire.

Today, Minco is one of the most active commercial real estate companies in Greater Lawrence, with the next generation heavily involved. Son, Lou, III and daughter, Christina are active full-time project managers, and son-in-law, Eric Loth, a recent MIT Real Estate Program graduate, has joined the firm in acquisitions and new ventures.

Minco's commitment to tradition and client satisfaction has never waivered. We believe that Greater Lawrence has a strong tradition of providing opportunities for hard working individuals and families. Our family is proud to be a part of this community and is grateful for the challenges and projects it has provided us.

MINCO
CORPORATION

Minco Corporation • 231 Sutton Street, North Andover, MA • 978-687-6200 • www.mincocorp.com

THE EAGLE-TRIBUNE

Since 1867

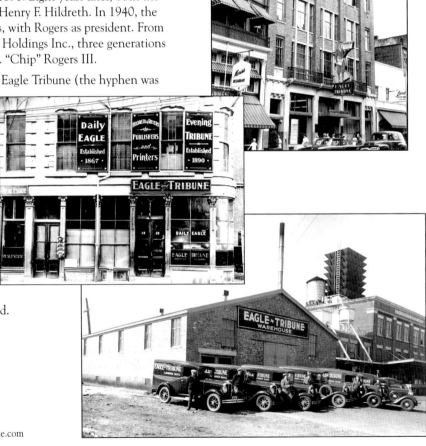

From its early days on Essex Street in Lawrence to its present home on Route 114 in North Andover, The Eagle-Tribune has been the newspaper of record for the Merrimack Valley.

On April 13, 1867, the first incarnation of the newspaper that would become The Eagle-Tribune was founded as the Essex Eagle at 153 Essex St. in Lawrence. A year later, the weekly newspaper became a morning daily newspaper and was renamed the Lawrence Daily Eagle.

As Greater Lawrence grew, the Evening Tribune was established in 1890. Eight years later, both the Eagle and the Tribune were purchased by Alexander H. Rogers and Henry F. Hildreth. In 1940, the Eagle-Tribune Publishing Co. took over operation of the newspapers, with Rogers as president. From 1942 to 2005, when the papers were sold to Community Newspaper Holdings Inc., three generations of the Rogers family served as publisher, with the last being Irving E. "Chip" Rogers III.

In 1959, the Eagle and the Tribune were combined as the Lawrence Eagle Tribune (the hyphen was added in 1969, when the nameplate was redesigned, adding the now familiar golden eagle. In November 1968, the newspaper moved to its new, state of the art plant on Route 114 at 100 Turnpike Street, North Andover.

It was on October 1, 1978, that The Eagle-Tribune made the leap to become a seven-day newspaper. Publisher Irving E. Rogers Jr. joined a group of reporters, editors and pressmen as the first edition of the new Sunday Eagle-Tribune rolled off the press.

Today, The Eagle-Tribune carries on the tradition of award-winning coverage of the region. The two-time Pulitzer Prize-winning newspaper has expanded far beyond its Essex Street origins. Today eagletribune.com and its associated websites, mobile sites and smart phone apps deliver millions of page views each month to informed readers in Massachusetts, New Hampshire and the world.

The Eagle-Tribune. join the discussion.

100 Turnpike Street, North Andover, MA 01845 – 978-946-2000 • eagletribune.com

INDEX

A

Abate, Mary, 125
Abbot Academy, Andover, 91
Abdallah, Monica, 129
Adams, Shirley, 60
aerial views, 36, 43, 112, 133
Ahearn, John, 64
Ahearn, William Henry, 40
Air Show poster, Haverhill, 15
aircraft, 15, 28, 99
Akimchuck, James, 84
Albach, Laurie, 124, 132
Alcarese, Ann, 78
Aldonis, James, 104
Aldonis, Jim, 70
Alexander Bruce School,
    Lawrence, 84
Allen, Daniel, 104
Allied Shoe Machinery bus,
    Haverhill, 82, 83
American Legion Auxiliary No. 34,
    Plaistow, 100
American Legion Hall, Lawrence,
    10
American Legion Post 219, North
    Andover, 46
Anderson, Alberta, 14
Anderson, H., 84
Anderson, Harold, 14
Andover
    aerial view, 43
    Christmas decorations, 37
    hurricane damage, 86, 87
    parades, 33, 106
    police department, 75, 93, 111
    street scenes, 42, 75, 134
    World War I Auditorium, 32
    *See also specific schools, social
    groups, and businesses*
Andover High School cheerleaders,
    101
Andrew, Charles, 60
Annaldo, Frank, 25
Anton, Alex, 126
Anton, Arthur, 126
Anton, John, 126

Anton, Sox, 126
Antone, Philip, 125
Antoon, Sam, 12
A&P store, Andover, 113
A&P store, Plaistow, 106
Argyle, Rev. George, 102
Arlington Mills Band of Lawrence, 8
Arraj, Debra, 129
Arsenault, Michelle, 129
Arthur H. DuGrenier Co., Haverhill,
    10
Arvanitis, George W., 128
Ashe, Gertrude P., 26
Ashford School, Methuen, 125
Ashford, Timmy, 100
Ashworth, Ada, 64
Assad, Joe, 12
Atkins, Barbara, 29
Atkins, Gilbert N., 39
Aufiero, Jayne, 132
Autieri, Elaine, 129
automobiles, 24, 53, 107
Ayer Mills war bond drive, 21

B

Baggett, James F., 26
Baggett, Joseph, 125
Baker, Carolyn, 84
Baker, David M., 130
Baker, Paula, 125
Balsamo, Gasper, 25
Balsamo, Grace, 20
Balsamo, Nellie, 20, 74
Baptist Church, Andover, 48
Barbagallo, Carman, 126
Barbagallo, Frank, 126
Barker, Diane, 60
Barker, Nellie, 30
Barone, Joe, 8
Barone, Tico, 8
Barone, Tony, 8
Barrett, Owen, 84
Barry, Susan, 124, 132
Bartolotta, Sebastian, 40
Bartula, Beatrice, 64
baseball teams

Bolta Co. champion team, 44
Boys Club, Lawrence, 25
Lawton's Hot Dog Stand team,
    76
Little League, Haverhill, 89
Mother and Son Baseball Game,
    Plaistow, 115
North Andover Community
    Center Team, 80
'Park Street Gang,' 89
South Lawrence West Browns
    Little League team, 70
St. Anthony's Church CYO, 12
UTWA baseball champions, 70
basketball teams, 44, 84, 102
Basso, Ella, 28
Batal, Vivian, 73
Bateman, Gertrude, 76
Bateman, Robert, 70
Battiato, Rose, 60
Batty, Mildred, 73
Bay State Merchants National Bank
    Christmas party, 73
Beals, Bernice, 64, 116
Bean, Fred, 73
Beauchamp, Michael, 125
Beaudoin, William, 44
Beaumont, Mary, 125
Bedard and Laroche Grocery
    Store, South Lawrence, 43
Bedard, Mr., 43
Beek, Harriet, 46
Bella, Angela, 52
Bella, Connie, 52
Bella, Joe, 52
Bellia, Nina, 60
Bellotti, Francis X., 128
Benedict, George, 66
Bennett, Barbara, 64, 110
Bennett, Bernice, 64, 116
Bennett, Fred, Jr., 116
Berger, Rosalind, 84
Bergeron, Ronald, 129
Berman, Marilyn E., 130
Bernardin, Richard, 125
Berry, Linda, 132
Berthel, Cheryl, 64, 110
Berthel, Delores, 60
Berthel, Marjory, 64
Berube, Norman 'Butch,' 110
Beshara, Abe, 12
bicycle-decorating event, North
    Andover, 63
Bier, Evelyn, 78
Bishop, Max, 44
Bistany, Claire, 126
Bixby, Ben, 57
Blanchette, James, 84
Blanchette, Peter, 124

Blessed Julie Billiart celebration,
    98
Blinn, Barbara, 126, 129
block party in Lawrence, 20
Blouin, Paul, 125
Bobek, Jacqueline, 84
Bodenrader, Louise, 124, 132
Boediner, Grace, 22
Bolta Co. baseball team, Lawrence,
    44
Bon Secours Hospital, Methuen,
    36
Bonaccorsi, Diane, 129
Borelli, Al, 25
Borelli, Barbara, 24
Botsch, William F., 44
Bottai, Joe, 107
Bourassa, Donna, 125
Bourassa, Kenneth, 125
Bouvier, Jacqueline, 125
Bower, Arthur, 76
Bower, George, 76
Bowes, Gertrude, 84
Bowman, Charles, 134
boxing, 12
Boy Scout Troops, 27, 33, 97
Boyd, Joe, 107
Boyle, Peter, 125
Boys Club, Lawrence, 22, 25
Bradford, Sacred Hearts Grammar
    School, 57
Bradley, John, 129
Bradley, Tom, 60
Brady, Virginia, 128
Bragg, Will, 59
Bramhill, Ronald, 24
Branco, Salvatore, 60
Brasseur, Beverly Ann, 130
Brasseur, Donald R., 77, 83
Brasseur, Elaine Sue, 83
Brassuer, Herbert, 130
Bread and Roses Parade,
    Lawrence, 116
Breen, Gertrude, 22
Bresnahan, Brendan, 60
Bresnahan, John, 128
Bresnahan, Mary, 124
Bresnahan, Patricia, 132
Bretton, Denise, 125
Bride, James, 66
Bride, John, 66
Brindle, Edward, 129
Broadhead, Raymond, 94
Broadhurst, Joan, 78
Broderick, Monsignor John F., 129
Brooks, Charles, 124
Brooks, Josephine Mangione, 13
Brown, Rev. Ernest, 94
Brown, John, 126

Brown, Liz, 51
Brown, Marion, 100
Brownie Troops, 102, 126
Brown's Diner, Methuen, 131
Bryant, Bernice, 32
Buckley, John J., 47, 114, 117,
    122
Buczko, Ted, 128
Bulmer, Daniel, 129
Burdin, Robert, 129
Burdin, Sheila, 129
Burgiel, Leslie, 66
Burke, Audrey, 60
Burke, Dorothea, 126
Burke, Maureen, 126, 129
Burke, Rt. Rev. Monsignor Joseph
    P., 129
Burnham, Freddy, 61
Burnham, Mrs., 64
Burns, Elizabeth, 129
Burns, Philip, 44
Burns, Sharon, 129
Burton, Ruth, 73
Buss, James H., 134

C

Cadagan, Mr., 40
Caffery, Claire, 60
Caffrey, Pat, 60
Cain, Patricia, 129
Calderone, Paula May, 125
Cali, Carmela, 60
Callahan, Andy, 12
Callahan, Edward, 22
Callahan, Shirley, 106
Campbell, Dave, 57
Camuso, Howard, 129
Canty, Jack, 25
Caraldi, Caryn, 124, 132
Carney, Neil, 125
Carroll, Ames, 29
Carrozza, Peter, 129
Carter, Lynne, 129
Carter, Malvina, 95
Caruso, Joe, 126
Caruso, Josie, 126
Casale, Georgie 'Babe,' 25
Casey, Ann, 132
Casey, Timothy, 124
Catalano, Catherine, 13
Catalano's Market, Lawrence, 58
Cavileri, Jim 'Cav,' 25
Celtin, Edward, 130
Centennial celebration, Haverhill,
    95
Centennial Parade, North Andover,
    94
Central School, Methuen, 71
Cestrone, Anthony, 60

Chaff, Clarence, 127
Chaff, William, Sr., 8
Chamberlain, Robert J., 100
Chamberlin, Francis, 80, 101
Chamberlin, Joseph, 80
Chapman, Ralph, 57
Chase, Bob, 104
Chase, John, 80
Chase, Paul, 130
Cheas, Kathryn, 84
cheerleaders, 31, 101, 103
Chernosky, Mary, 129
Christie, Andrew, 31
Cities Service Station, Lawrence,
    110
Cleary, Harold, 128
Clement, Don, 44
Clement, Martin, 124
Clement, Theresa, 132
Cloutier, Sharon, 125
Cockroft, Joe, 76
Coco, Joyce, 129
Cole, Arthur, 134
Coleman, Bea, 73
Coleman, Harold, 73
Coleman, Jimmy, 77, 83, 98,
    101, 131
Coleman, Marian, 77, 131
Coleman, Michael, 98, 131
Coleman, Nancy, 77, 98, 131
Coleman, Walter J., 9, 62, 77,
    131
Collins, Irene, 52
Collins, Mark, 101
Collins, Maurice 'Jake,' 44
Collopy, Laurence, 84
Concanon, Joan, 129
Condurelli, William, 25
Connelly, Michael, 125
Connors, Deborah, 129
Connors, Karen, 124, 132
Conradsen, Dorothy, 46
Consentino, Laura, 124
Consentino, Roseanne, 129
Consentino, Teresa, 132
Constantineau, Donna, 124, 132
Cordeau, Jeanette, 26
Corkery, Raymond F., 134
Cormier, Rachel, 45
Costello, James, 57
Crabtree, Tom, 25
Craddock, Kevin, 125
Crompton, Kim, 132
Cronin, Charles, 21
Cronshaw, William H., 134
Crosdale, Fred, 73
Cross, Georgette, 73
Crossman, Marjorie, 60
Croteau, Dick, 76

Crouch, Beatrice, 64
Cub Scout troop, Lawrence, 101
Cullen, Connie, 100
Cunningham, Nancy, 132
Curran, Elizabeth, 104
Currant, Thomas, 104
Cutter, Tommy, 101
Cyr, Johnnie, 25

D

Dadducci, Josie, 126
Dadducci, Linda, 124, 132
Daigault, Alan, 84
Daignault, Emil, 107
Dainouski, Donna, 110
Danahy, Timothy, 70
Dane, John P., 130
Daniels, Ralph, 31
Davis & Furber Textile Machinery
    float, Lawrence, 120
Davis, Albert, 106
Davis, Mabel, 106
Dawaliby, James, 124
Deacy, Michael, 70
Dean, Ruth, 24
DeBurro, Carl, 25
DeBurro, Catherine Catalano, 13
DeCourcey, Judith, 60
Defazio, Charles, 134
Delaney, Regis, 60
DeLucia, Karen, 129
DeMauro, Maire, 60
DeMonaco, Joseph, 25
Denault, Ora, 100
Denuzzio, Albert, 125
Dequattro, Carl, 44
Desaulnier, Edward J., 134
Deschamps, Irene, 84
Desrosiers, Arthur, 60
Detora, Leighton, 80
Dever, Paul, 47
Devine, Chris, 122
Devine, Emma, 122
Devine, Jim, 77
Devine, Steve, 77
DiDio, Marie, 132
Dillon, B., 84
Diorio, Linda, 125
DiPaolo, Sally, 38
DiPrima, Brenda, 126
DiPrima, Dominic, 126
DiPrima, Marcia, 126
DiPrima, Rose, 126
DiSalvo, Deborah, 129
DiSalvo, Nancy, 129
Divaney, Timothy, 124
Doherty, Jackie, 25
Don Sully's Swingsters, 38
Donaghue Elementary School,

Merrimac, 100
Donahue, Collette, 132
Donohue, Donna, 125
Donovan, Christopher, Jr., 117
Donovan, Christopher M., 88, 117
Donovan, Jane, 116
Donovan, Michael, 117
Dooley, Maureen, 132
Dowling, Pamela, 116
Dowling, Peter, 125
Downing, Annabel, 100
Downing, Mary, 100
Downs, Bernice Bryant, 32
Doyon, Jerry, 44
Doyon, Leo, 44
Doyon, Ray 'Shorty,' 44
Driver, G. Hudson, 78
Drouin, Paul, 104
Drummond, Arthur, 80
Drummond Playground, North
    Andover, 63, 101
Ducheneau, Bob, 76
Ducheneau, Eugene, 84
Duggan, Catherine, 122
Duggan, Constance, 46
Duggan, Jimmy, 122
Duggan, Margie, 60
Duggan, Mary Geraghty, 79
Durkin, Charles, 60
Durso, Marie, 66
Dussault, Phillip, 124
Dutton Airport, Haverhill, 133
Dutton, Dave, 99
Dutton, Diane, 99
Dutton, Donald, 99
Dutton, Howard, 15, 28, 99
Dwindells, Elizabeth, 132
Dwindells, Veronica, 132
Dwyer, Gertrude Breen, 22
Dyer, Dennis, 125
Dyleski, Joan, 60

E
Ead, Fred, 12
Eagle-Tribune
    about, 140
    dedication of new building, 131
    newsroom, 9
    Old Gold Cigarettes memorabilia,
        64
    submarine in front of, 14
Earley, Alberta, 24
East Junior High School, Andover,
    134
Ebert, Deborah, 129
Edson, June, 51
Eilkerson, Jack, 25
Eisenhower, Dwight D., 69
Elander, May, 52

Elander's Men's Shop, Andover,
    40, 48
Eldred, Kathleen, 60
Elks Club Lady Elks induction, 106
Ellen Elizabeth, Sr., 132
Elliot, Bruce, 80
Elliott's sale, Haverhill, 82
Ellis, Francis, 107
Ellis, Kathleen, 129
Elston, Bernie, 122
Emmons, Barbara, 66
English, Raymond, 129
Enire, Henry, 93
Enman, William, 125
Erving, John M., 134
Evangelos, Nick, 25

F
Facela, Nadine, 132
Fairweather, Connie, 16
Fallon, Beverly, 125
fashion show, 65
Faul, Norbert, 127
Fay, Deborah, 129
Fay, Susan, 125
Feast of the Three Saints,
    Lawrence, 92
Federico, Kathryn, 125
Feinman, Andy, 123
Feinman, Freya, 84
Fenton, Patricia, 104
Fielding, Albert, 102
Fielding, Walter, 102
Fillipon, Debra, 129
Finacharo, Mary, 60
Finneran, William, 94
Finnigan, Sharon, 132
Fiore, Augustine, 129
Fiore, Linda, 84
fire departments, 56, 100
Fire, William, 84
fires, 20, 88
First Baptist Church, Haverhill, 118
First Church of the Nazarene,
    Haverhill, 72
First Methodist Church members,
    North Andover, 45
Fisichella, Constance, 13
Fisichella, Josephine, 13
Fisichelli, Gloria, 24
Fitzgerald, Mary Beth, 125
Fitzpatrick, Kay, 100
Flathers, Mary, 84
Fleischman, J., 84
Fleming, John, 84
Fletcher, Everett, 73
Flynn, Arthur, 12
Foley, Daniel, 125
Foley, Vincent, 127

football teams, 12, 44, 52, 102
Ford, Martha, 125
Foster, Alan, 80
Foster, Marilyn, 126, 129
Fournier, Richard, 70
Fourth of July Parade, Lawrence,
    19
Fraser, Suzanne, 66
Frechette, Paul, 129
Friedrich, Esther, 46
Frost School dedication, 111

G
Gabriel, Scotty, 12
Gaffney, Edward, 125
Gagne, Irene, 84
Gallant, Jacqueline, 60
Gallipeau, Leo, 107
Galloway, Ruth, 73
Gardella's Fruit Store, 82
Garfi, Donna, 125
Garofalo, Annmarie, 13
Garofalo, Domenic 'Dick' 'Garry,'
    26, 38
Garofalo, Josephine, 13
Garofalo, Santa 'Sally' 'Babes'
    Sapia, 26, 38
Garvey, Bob, 44
Garvis, Paula, 132
Gasarunas, Rev., 122
Gavribuk, Walter, 70
Gearin, Mareen, 125
Gebow, Marilyn, 100
Gelt, George, 74
George Gelt's market, Salem, 74
Geraci, Joanne, 84
Geraghty, Mary, 79
Gibbons, Thomas, 84
Gilbert E. Hood School, Lawrence,
    90
Gilbert, Roy, 73
Giles, Beth, 102
Giles, Dorothy Moore, 68, 102
Giles, Frank S., 68, 69, 79, 114
Giles, Scott, 84, 102
Gilligan, Martin, 134
Gilman, Donna, 106
Gilman, Mary, 51
Gilmore, William, 104
Girouard, Annee Marie, 132
Glover, Bernice, 51
God and Country Parade,
    Lawrence, 119, 120, 121
Goddard, Ruth, 73
Godfrey, Ruth, 52
Godin, Robert, 125
Goffstein, Bernard, 114
Goings, Joe, 107
Golan, Marilyn, 73

Golden, John, 125
Golden, Pat, 101, 103
Gonet, E., 84
Gonet, J., 84
Goodrich, Gerald E., 31
Goodsell, Barbara, 60
Gosselin, Bobby, 89
Gosselin, Ray, 89
Gosselin, Tommy, 25
Gould, Mary Ellen, 84
Goulet, Robert, 117
Graham, Dolores, 24
Graham, Fran, 128
Graham, James, 129
Graham, Lee Ann, 126
Grant's Department Store,
    Lawrence, 111
Greenwood, Eileen, 46
Greenwood, Warren, 47
Greole, Donald, 60
Grieco Brothers party, Lawrence,
    74
Griffin, Debbie, 125
Griffin, Paul, 125
Grogan's Playground, North
    Andover, 89
Guido, Charles, 70
Guillemette, Ray, 107
Guilmette, Dennis, 125
Guilmette, Jerry, 15, 16, 110
Guilmette, Kay, 16, 24, 110
Gullar, Arlene, 73
Guthrie, Michael, 101
Guthrie, Thomas, 125
Guy, Pauline, 125

H
Hadley, Richard F., 134
Haigh, Lois, 60
Hajjar, Bonita, 124
Hajjar, Doreen, 124, 132
Hamblet employees picnic,
    Methuen, 63
Hamilton, Wayne, 84
Hammond, Joan, 66
Hanlon, Jane, 125
Hanson, Helen, 66
Harb, David, 125
Harb, Edward, 12
hardware store, Haverhill, 58
Harriman, Betty, 66
Hart, Charles F., 54, 127
Hart, Gert, 73
Hart, Joan, 124
Hart, Virginia, 46
Hartwig, Nettie, 116
Hashem, John, 12
Hassey, Phyllis, 84
Hatem, Edward, 12

Hatton, Mrs. Robert, 52
Haverhill
    aerial views, 112, 133
    bus driver, 67
    Centennial celebration, 95
    Little League baseball team, 89
    street scenes, 53, 96, 97, 118,
        131, 133
    Water Street fire, 88
    See also specific schools, social
        groups, and businesses
Haverhill High School, 9, 29, 57,
    61, 67
Haverhill Rotary Club 30th
    anniversary, 31
Haverhill Savings Bank vault, 114
Hay, Alan, 24
Hayes, Eileen, 73
Hayes, Jeannette, 73
Hayes, John, 73, 134
Hayes, Michael J., 105
Hayes, Phyllis, 73, 116
Healy, Thomas, 84
Hec and Joe's Diner, Haverhill, 93
Heffner, Joelle, 125
Heil, Doris, 51
Heil, Louis, 51
Helbick, Therese, 129
Helen Julia, Sr., 129
Henneley, John 'Pat,' 44
Hennessey, James, 84
Hering, Gustave, 127
Herliky, Mike, 73
Hershfield, Doris, 84
Herter, Christian A., 68, 69
Herward, Mary Jean, 60
Hewett, Mareen, 125
Hickel, Patricia, 124
Hickey, Margaret, 73
Hickey, Raymond, 75
Hideriotis, John Michael, 46
Hien, Robert, 24
Higgins, Mr., 60
Highland View Farm, 110
Hill, Barbara, 60
Hill, Gladys, 52
Hill, Kathleen, 126, 129
Hill, Mona, 126
Hill, Peggy, 78
Hill, Robin, 126
Hillard, Richard, 129
Hillis, Bob, 102
Hillon, Charles, 75
Hilton, Elizabeth, 88
Hilton, Henry L., 88, 106
Hilton, Leona, 88
Hilton, Lester, 88

Hinton, Irving, 73
Hoegen, Jim, 102
Holland, Patricia, 125
Holmes, Francis, 84
Holmes, Thelma 'Ginger,' 100
Holt, Maureen, 125
Holtham, John, 125
Holy Rosary Church, Lawrence,
    13, 26
Holy Rosary procession, 40
Holy Rosary School May
    Procession, 13
home moving process, 113
Hosley, Carlton R., 134
Houghton, Father, 95
Houle, Frank, 107
Houle, Henry, 107
Houle, Rosemary, 84
Hovey, Lewis R., 31
Hovey, Martin R., 31
Howard, Beverly, 46
Howard, John, 102
Howard Rams sandlot football
    team, 44
Howard, Sandra, 102
Howes, Anne, 66
Hubley, Wallace, 31
Hulub, Paul, 25
Hunter, Marjorie, 128
Huntress, Barbara, 100
Huot, Ray, 76
Hurricane Carol damage, 86, 87
Hussey, Kathleen, 124
Hymanson, Marjorie, 84

I
Ianazzo, John, 25
Ilano, George, 111
Incropera, Francis, Sr., 111
Incropera, Frank, 108, 127
Indian Chief motorcycle, 77
Ingalls, Eleanor, 100
Ingalls, Harriet, 100
Ingalls, Roger, 79
Ingalls, Virginia, 100
Innes, Duane, 122
Innes, Grace, 17
Innes, Kevin, 122
Innes, Robert, 122

J
Jackman, Mary Jane, 102
Jackson, Gail, 125
Jackson, Robert, 129
Jackson, Skip, 89
Jacobs, Roland, 24
Jacques, Alcide G., 130
Jacques Bros. Barber Shop,

Lawrence, 130
Jacques, Gedeon 'Gene,' 130
Jampens, Doris, 78
Jarosz, Marilyn, 125
Jean, Ron, 107
Jellison, Muriel, 46
Jennings, Bob, 76
Jiadosz, Elaine S., 76, 83
Jimenez, Pedro, 129
Joery, Sylvia, 73
John Breen School, Lawrence, 60
Johnson, Barbara, 46
Johnson Cottage hurricane
    damage, 87
Johnson, Evelyn, 46
Johnson, Frank, 24
Johnson, George H., 134
Johnson High School, North
    Andover, 24, 76, 85
Johnson, Theodore R., 134
Johnson, Walter
Johnson, Wilfred, 56, 110
Joncas, Arthur, 107
Joncas, Lucien, 107
Jones, Joanne, 24
Joseph Pulvina's orchestra, 45
Jowdy, Edward, 12
Judson, Fr. Paul, 116
Julie Peter, Sr., 132
Junior/Senior Proms, 85, 90
Juniper Park, Methuen, 63
Junkins, Ilene, 84
Juras, Rev., 122

K
Kannheiser, George, 70, 104
Kaplan, Robert, 84
Karabashian, Irene, 73
Karolunos, Carol, 60
Kartaros, George K., 130
Kasheta, Nancy, 124, 132
Kay, Bunny, 73
Kazanjian, Harold, 125
Keenan, Charles, 100
Keezer, Dorothy, 51
Keezer, Joan, 51
Keleher, Augustine, 127
Kellan, Robert, 84
Kelley, Neil, 129
Kelly, Father, 129
Kelly, Shirley, 46
Kennedy, Gloria, 60
Kennedy, John F., 69
Kennedy, Margaret, 31
Kennedy, Ted, 116, 120
Kenney, Jean, 129
Kettinger, Charles, 84
Khory, Carol, 125
Kibildis, Norma, 84

Kilcourse, Patrick, 80
Kiley, Daniel P., 40, 62
Kimball, Pamela, 102
King, John, 134
Kinsella, Rayma, 116
Kirk, Arthur, 94
Kirkman, Valerie, 129
Kirsch, David, 125
Klien, Billy, 24
Klier, Deborah, 125
Knightly, Carl, 40
Knightly, Janey, 89
Knipe Bros. shoe factory, Haverhill, 96
Kobos, John, 44
Koerner, Frederick, 129
Korbey, Brenda, 129
Korsak, Joseph, 44
Koza, Henry, 76
Krikorian, Arthur, 125
Kryda, Julius, 122
Kyle, Wilber J., 82

L

LaBranche, Christine, 102
LaCharitie, Rene, 126
Ladd, David, 51
Lafond, Evelyn, 104
Laliberte, Alfred, 134
Lambert, Joseph J. 'Bob,' 123
Lamour, Dorothy, 22
Landman's Field, Plaistow, 115
Landry, Beulah, 51
Landry, Phyllis, 51
Lane, Thomas, 47, 69
Lane, William, 125
Lannon, Bill, 125
Lanory, Stella, 73
Laplume, Regina, 100
Laratonda, Frances, 129
Larkin, Eldred, 134
Laroche, Donat, 43
Larson, Betty, 73
Latulippe, Richard, 70
Laudani, Mary, 73
Laudani, Paul, 124
Lavery, John, 129
Lavigne, Gloria, 46
Lavoie, Carol, 129
Lavoie, Robert, 129
Lawrence
  aerial view, 36
  baseball teams, 25, 70
  block party, 20
  fire department, 100
  Mt. Vernon Veterans Housing Project groundbreaking, 49
  police department, 40, 62, 88, 127
  school safety patrol, 108
  street scenes, 58, 88, 93, 112, 126
  submarine in, 14
  UTWA baseball champions, 70
  Wood Mill presentations, 10
  World War II events, 35, 49
  See also Lawrence parades; *specific schools, social groups, and businesses*
Lawrence Centennial Parade, 54, 78, 79
Lawrence Common, World War II statue dedication on, 49
Lawrence Daily Eagle employees, 40
Lawrence Days shopping, 111
Lawrence Democratic Headquarters, 128
Lawrence General Hospital School of Nursing students, 46
Lawrence High School, 12, 31, 62, 102, 105
Lawrence parades
  Bread and Roses Parade, 116
  Centennial Parade, 54, 78, 79
  Fourth of July Parade, 19
  God and Country Parade, 119, 120, 121
Lawrence Railroad Depot, 15
Lawrence Redevelopment Authority, 126
Lawrence Stadium outing, 34
Lawrence, Walter E., 130
Lawton's Hot Dog Stand baseball team, 76
Le Branc, Barbara, 60
Leary, Lois, 79
Lebowitz, Alan, 84
LeBrecque, Dennis, 84
LeClair, Ginny, 51
LeClair, Gloria, 51
Lee, David, 129
Lee, Dougie, 25
Lee, George 'Benny,' 25
Lefebre, Eva, 84
LeFleur, Richard, 125
Legge, Pauline, 51
Legunas, M., 105
Lehne, Arthur S., 130
Leith, Ruth, 100
Leland, Lucy, 66
Leonard, Bryan, 134
Leonard, Eleanor, 60
Leone, Thomas, 127
Lepine, Armand J., 134
Letendre, Stephen, 125
LeVasseur, Alan, 84
Libby, Gladys, 100

Lippe, Leo, 70
L'Italien, John, 129
Lithuanian Citizen's Club, 105, 122
Little League baseball team, Haverhill, 89
Lodge, Henry Cabot, 69
Lombardo, Richard, 104
Long, Phil, 25
Longworth, William, 68
Look Photography, Andover, 59
LoPiano, Margaret Kennedy, 31
Lord, Barbara, 60
Lord, Russell, 73
Lucchesi, Elena, 124, 132
Luistro, Ruth, 24
Lurnari, Tony, 60
Lynch, Justine, 24
Lynch, Karen, 124

M

Maccarone, Felicia, 132
MacGilvrey, John, 60
MacMillan, Rev. Archibald, 17
Madden, Rev. Father, 57
Magee Lodge, Raymond, 97
Maguire, Vincent, 70
Mailloux, Donat 'Joe,' 43
Mailloux, Isabelle, 100
Mailloux, Joe, 41
Malcolm, Fred, 114
Mallen, Pamela, 129
Malori, Marie, 132
Mandros, Cynthia, 84
Mangione, Josephine, 13
Maniscalo, Frances, 125
Mann, Al, 73
Mann, Douglas, 101
Mann, Walter, 73
Manning, Brian, 129
Mansour, Lorice, 46
Marcello, Carolyn, 129
Marcello, Phillip, 129
Marconi, Bobby, 90
Marie Charles, Sr., 132
Marie Roberts, Sr., 129
Marincelli, Steven, 124
Marino, Angelo, 126
Marisola, Joe, 107
Marsden, Charles, 129
Martin, Ron, 102
Martin, Shane, 124
Martone, Leila, 124
Martone, Lelia, 132
Mary Rose, Sr., 132
Masoud, Thomas, 129
Massachusetts Legislative Textile Commission, 68
Massachusetts State Guard, North Andover unit, 14

Matchead, Andy, 73
Matson, Cheryl, 102
Mawson, Arthur, 44
May Queens and attendants, 13, 104
Maynard, Raymond, 40
McAvoy, Frank, 44
McCarthy, John, 44
McColbe, Grace Boediner, 22
McCollum, Edith, 52
McCormick, Joanne, 125
McGowan, John, 24
McGowan, Phillip, 124
McGregor, Bill, 89
McGregor, George E., 130
McGuire, Barbara, 125
McGuire, Dennis, 125
McGuire, Joseph E., 128
McGurn, Scott, 129
McHugh, Suzanne, 84
McIntyre, Jack, 80
McIntyre, Tom, 80
McKay, William, 129
McKenna, Mary Jane, 124, 132
McKewen, Cynthia, 51
McKone, John, 95
McMahon, Norma, 78
McNamara, Raymond V., 31, 130
McPhee, Catherine, 60
McQuade Library, North Andover, 133
Mechanics Blocks, Lawrence, 126
Meehan, Claudia, 22
Meehan, David, 125
Meehan, Gertrude P., 26
Meehan, James, 22, 26, 49
Meehan, Mrs. James I, 106
Melincoff, Jack, 22
Memorial Day Parade, 100
Memorial Day Parades, 106
Menihan, Dan, 24
Mercier, Norman, 44
Merrimac, Donaghue Elementary School students, 100
Merrimack College, McQuade Library, North Andover, 133
Merrimack Ice Co. fire, 20
Merrimack National Bank, Haverhill, 37
Merrimack Valley Mems III names
Merrow, Everett, 73
Mershon, Herbert B., 130
Mesrobian, John, 129
Messier, Roberta, 84
Messina, Charles, 125
Messina, Mary, 13
Methuen
  Bon Secours Hospital, 36
  legislative delegation, 68

Santa and children, 73
Washington Monument, 95, 104
See also specific schools, social groups, and businesses
Methuen Auxiliary Police, 127
Methuen High School, 38, 84
Methuen Memorial Music Hall, 118
Methuen Women's Republican Club, 68
Meyer, Marie, 60
Michalewicz, Francis, 129
Michelle, Sister, 125
Midore, Arlene, 84
Miller, Reid, 102
Milnes, Chris, 89
Mimno, Margaret, 125
Minco Development Corp., 139
Minicucci, Peter, 30
Mistretta, Grace Balsamo, 20
Mitchell, Walter P., 134
Mitchell's Department Store, Haverhill, 59
Model Store, Haverhill, 48
Modeler's Haven, Lawrence, 123
Moderne Shoppe, Methuen, 117
Mondale, Madeline, 52
Monroe, Ray, 24
Moore, Dorothy, 68
Moore, Horace 'Mitt,' 102
Moore, Jean, 51
Moore, Rod, 44
Moran, Gillie, 76
Morgan, Forrest Neville, 67
Morin, Paula, 125
Morrison, Judith, 124
Morrison, Judy, 132
Morton, Susanne, 102
Moses, Lisa, 126
Mother and Son Baseball Game, Plaistow, 115
motorcycle policeman, Andover, 93
Mottram, Barbara, 84
Mt. Vernon Veterans Housing Project groundbreaking, Lawrence, 49
Muller, Thelma, 122
Munroe, Dorothy, 52
Murach Brothers Orchestra, 8
Murphy, Catherine, 46
Murphy, Cornelia, 46
Murphy, John, 104, 130
Murphy, Maureen, 124
Murphy, Michael, 82
Murphy, Robert, 70
Musk, Priscilla, 73
Muzerall, Bobby, 83
Myers, Anna, 122
Myers, Claire, 84
Myers, Clary, 122

N

Napier, George C., 134
Napolitano, Bill, 73
Nardone, Michael, 25
Nardone, Phillip, 25
Neel, Colleen, 132
Neilon, John, 84
Neketuk, Mike, 25
Nelson, Susan, 110
New England Telephone and Telegraph Co. float, Lawrence, 120
New York World's Fair, 8
Newall, George, 73
Newman, Harriet, 52
"Night with Robert Burns," United Presbyterian Church, Lawrence, 17
'Nite Club,' YMCA, 30
Nicolosi, Joseph, 125
Nolan, Rosemary, 129
Norcia, Dot, 126
Nordengren, Edward M., 130
Norris, Reid, 25
North Andover
  bicycle-decorating event, 63
  Centennial Parade, 94
  Drummond Playground, 63, 101
  Grogan's Playground, 89
  Massachusetts State Guard unit, 14
  Stevens Memorial Library Story Hour, 115
  Waverly Playground, 80, 81
  See also specific schools, social groups, and businesses
North Andover Community Center Baseball Team, 80
North Andover Garden Club, 66
North Andover High School, 84, 90
North Parish Church congregation, North Andover, 81
Northern Essex Community College, 4, 135–38
Norwood, Ann, 66

O

O'Brien, Dave, 102
O'Brien, Mrs. Willard, 130
O'Claire, Patrica, 125
O'Connell, Bruce, 129
O'Donald, Robert, 124
O'Donnell, Mary Ellen, 132
O'Hearn, John, 22
Old Gold Cigarettes memorabilia, 64

Olenio, Bob, 25
O'Neil, James, 128
O'Neil, Linda, 132
Ordzie, Edmund, 44
Orr, Elaine, 84
Osgood, Benjamin, 80
Osgood, Gayton, 66
Osgood, John, 40
Osgood, Katherine, 66
O'Shea, John J., 31
Ouellette, Jerry, 70
Ouellette, Raymond, 70

P

Packard School, Lawrence, 60
Page, Stephanie, 102
Palermo, Patricia, 129
Palermo, Rose, 126
Palmer, Ruth, 116
Palmer, Thomas, 116
Panorelli, Agnes, 60
Panorelli, Annmarie Garofalo, 13
paperboys, 91
Paquette, Claire, 73
parades
  Boy Scouts in Andover parade, 33
  Centennial Parade, North Andover, 94
  Holy Rosary procession, 40
  Memorial Day Parades, 100, 106
  Plaistow Bicentennial, 51
  See also Lawrence parades
Pare, Diane, 124
Parent, Brian, 129
'Park Street Gang' baseball team, 89
Parrah, James, 104
Parrino, Claire, 124, 132
Parson Bernard House, 66
Parsons, Brackett, 134
Paulack, Thaddius, 124
Peabody, Chub, 128
Pedrick, Jack, 76
Penkus, U., 105
Pennisi, Cammy, 98, 104
Pennisi, Carmela, 46
Pennisi, Mario, 64
Pennisi, Sam, 46
Pepin, Christine, 129
Perillo, John, 129
Perrault, Bob, 102
Perricho, Anne Marie, 124
Perruchio, Sammy, 89
Perry, Gregory, 129
Peterson, Joyce, 84
Petkevich, E., 105
Petteruti, Americo A., 9

Petteruti, Josephine Garofalo, 13
Petteruti, Michael, 29
Phelps, Leila, 24
Piazza, Doreen, 125
Picone, Karen, 132
Pierce, Bob, 44
Pike School graduation dance, 66
Piper Cub, Haverhill, 99
Piskadlo, Chester, 44
Pitocchelli, Eleanore, 78
Pittochelli, Tina, 73
Pizzano, Ann Marie, 125
Plaistead, Ann, 66
Plaistow
    Bicentennial celebration, 51
    Brownie Troop, 102
    Landman's Field, 115
    Mother and Son Baseball Game,
        Plaistow, 115
    street scene, 36
    *See also specific schools, social
        groups, and businesses*
Plaistow Boys Athletic Basketball
    Team, 44
Pleasant Valley Farm, Methuen,
    20, 46
Poh, Jackie, 25
Poirier, Beverly, 125
police departments
    Andover, 75, 93, 111
    Lawrence, 40, 62, 88, 127
    Methuen Auxiliary Police, 127
Pomerleau, Lillian, 73
Poremba, Robert, 60
Porter, Stepheny, 102
Posternak, Joe, 123
Posternak's Kosher Market,
    Lawrence, 123
Poulin, Amos, 60
Poulin, Sandy, 84
Proulx, Eilleen, 73
Puglessi, Andrew, 24
Pulvina's orchestra, 45
Punchard High School, Andover
    Andover W.W.II veterans class,
        39
    Band, 32
    cheerleaders, 103
    dance at, 65
    football, 52, 103
    Girls Marching Band, 70
Pupillo, Nellie, 46
Puppularde, Grace, 73
Purcell, Thomas, 104
Putzig, Rev. Conrad, 116

Q

Quarterone, Denise, 129
Quintel, Ellen, 124

Quintel, Thomas, 124
Quirinale, Richard, 104

R

radio stations, 47, 67
railroad depots, 15, 96
Rainbow Girls (Masons), 57
Raineri, Anne, 24
Ramey, Lenny, 12
Ramskill, Arlene, 46
Rancourt, Doris, 46
Rancourt, Jean, 107
Rancourt, Robert, 60
Randall, George 'Sailor Joe,' 56
Randall, Ron, 107
Raymond, Rosemary, 73
Red Tavern, Methuen, 73
Reming, Dick, 84
Rennie, Don, 25
Rhodes, Ralph, 44
Richter, John, 73
Riley, Richard, 60
Rioux, Robert, 24
Rivet, Paul, 125
Robillard, Donna, 124
Robinson, Harry F., 41
Robinson, Mrs., 64
Rochussen, Bob, 44
Roddy, Steven, 125
Rogers, Alan, 73
Rogers, Arthur, 44
Rogers, Irving E., Jr., 64
Rogers, Linda, 124, 132
Rollins School, Lawrence, 24
Roosevelt, Franklin D., rally, 11
Rose Vincent, Sr., 132
Rosenberg, Michaela, 84
Rottler, Mary Lou, 125
Rowell, Cynthia, 102
Rowell, Katie, 115
Rozzi, Dickie, 89
Ruel, Mary-Jo, 132
Ruggerio, Cynthia, 129
Russell, Alwyn, 127
Russell, Jessie, 122
Russell, Richard, 129
Russo, Michael
Russo, Sarah, 13
Russus, Ray, 93
Rutter, Pete, 73
Ryan, Kevin, 107
Ryan, Patricia, 125
Ryan, William H. 'Billy,' 61

S

Saalfrank, George, 60
Sabbagh, Thomas, 129
Sacred Heart School, Lawrence,

28
Sacred Hearts Grammar School,
    Bradford, 57
Salach, David, 129
Salafia, Mr. and Mrs. John, 13
Salem, 37, 56, 74, 96
Sammataru, John, 73
Sanford, Alma, 46
Santa and children, Methuen, 73
Sapia, Santa 'Sally' 'Babes,' 26
Sapienza, Fred, 44
Saracusa, Linda, 125
Sarcione, Rosemary, 84
Sarto, Marie, 125
Scanlon, Dorothy, 78
Scanlon, Jack, 128
Scannell, Everett, 66
Scannell, Patricia, 129
Schoenfeld, Frances, 46
school safety patrol, Lawrence,
    108
Schuman, Madeline, 84
Scionte, Mary, 124, 132
Scire, Angela, 10, 16, 20, 74
Scire, Connie, 16
Scire, Joseph, 13, 16
Scire, Salvatore, 16
Scire, Sam, 16
scrap metal drive, 23
Scuderi, Rose, 13
Scuito, Marguerite, 116
Seabrook Beach, 117
Sean Marguerite, Sr., 132
Seed, Barbara, 132
Seguin, Richard, 70
Shawsheen Village, aerial view, 43
Shawsheen Women's Club,
    Andover, 66
Sheehy, Anne Mary, 132
Sheehy, Jack, 44
Sheehy, Jim, 44
Sherman, Louise, 52
Shupetris, A., 105
Siccerrollis, Peter, 24
Signor, Marilyn, 84
Silva, Bob, 44
Silva, Dolores, 84
Simon, Mary Jane, 31
Simpson, Stephanie, 125
Sirois, Arthur, 41, 43
Sirois, 'Babe,' 100
Sirois, 'Fat,' 100
Sirois, John, 126
Sirois, Mr. and Mrs. Honore, 100
Sirois, 'Pete,' 100
Sirois, René, 100
Slack, Thomas, 68
Smith, Bernard, 124
Smith, Bill, 73

Smith Chevrolet Co., Haverhill, 53
Smith, Fred R., 31
Smith, Jack, 107
Smith, Jimmy, 89
Smith, Joe, 89, 90
Smith, Larry, 128
Smith, Louise, 64
Solomon, Edmond, 12
Soper, William, 60
Soreff, Stuart, 84
Sorenson, Roberta, 102
South Church, Andover, 41, 52
South Lawrence Flooring Co., 107
South Lawrence West Browns Little
    League baseball team, 70
Southwick, Ed, 73
Sparks, Albert G., 134
Spirdione, Albert, 84
Spitaleri, Anthony, 60
St. Andrews's Church boys
    basketball team, 102
St. Anne's Drum Corps, 22
St. Anthony's Church CYO baseball
    team, 12
St. Augustine's May Procession,
    Lawrence, 83
St. Augustine's School, Lawrence,
    116, 125
St. Joseph's Grammar School,
    Haverhill, 45
St. Laurence O'Toole School,
    Lawrence, 115, 124, 132
St. Mark's Methodist Church, 64,
    110, 116
St. Mary's Boy Scout Troop,
    Lawrence, 27
St. Mary's Church, Lawrence,
    98, 119
St. Mary's High School, Lawrence,
    85, 104
St. Monica's School, Methuen,
    126, 129
St. Patrick's Church May Queen
    and attendants, Lawrence, 104
St. Patrick's Grammar School,
    Lawrence, 129
Stankatis, Donald, 80
Staples, Henry, 70
Sterns, Charlie, 61
Stevens, Frances, 100
Stevens Memorial Library Story
    Hour, North Andover, 115
Stevens Mill, North Andover, 29
Stillman, Howell, 73
street scenes
    Andover, 42, 75, 134
    Haverhill, 53, 96, 97, 118,
        131, 133
    Lawrence, 58, 88, 93, 112,

126
Stundza, John, 122
Stundzia, Matilda, 105
submarine in Lawrence, 14
Sullivan, Anna, 90
Sullivan, Jack, 25
Sullivan, Janice, 129
Sullivan, Joe, 128
Sullivan, John, 125
Sullivan, Judith, 125
Sullivan, Marian, 128
Sullivan, Ray, 25
Sullivan, Rosemary, 132
Sunderland, Arthur, 73
Sutcliffe, Diane, 60
Swingsters, Don Sully's, 38
Szostak, Kenneth, 129

T

Takesian, Charles, 125
Tardugno, Marilyn, 129
Tartaglione, Louis, 128
Veroneau, Ada, 51
Tasty Fine Do-Nut Co., Haverhill,
    46
Taylor, Douglas, 84
Taylor, J. Kenneth, 128
Taylor, Linda, 84
Tessitore, Anthony, 24
Theresa St. Joseph, Sr., 129
Theriault, Norman, 84
Therrien, Michael, 125
Thesse, Bob, 102
Thomas, Elsie, 84
Thomas, G. Lefty, 25
Thomas, Maureen, 124, 132
Thorton's Valley Oil Co., Haverhill,
    72
Thwaite, Charles, 18
Thwaite, Thomas, 18
Thwaites Market, Methuen, 18
Tilton School, Haverhill, 90
Tinkham, Bill, 44
Tinkham, David, 24, 44
Tinkham, Patricia, 24
Toher, Jean, 125
Tony Brown Orchestra, 8, 103
Touma, Joe, 12
Touma, Tony, 12
Tozier, Alan, 93
Tozier, Anna, 102
Traynor, Christine, 132
Traynor, Mary Lou, 125
Trignani, Roland, 25
Trinitarian Congregational Church
    choir, North Andover, 31
Trombley, Bob, 44
Trombley, Dick, 44
Truman, Harry S., 47, 69
Truman, Margaret, 47, 69

Trumble, Richard C., 130
Trumbull, Bertha, 46
Turcotte, Hector, 84
Turkey Town Trotters, North
    Andover, 128
Tyer Rubber Co., Andover
    factory, 114
    fashion show, 65

U

United Formal, 35
United Presbyterian Church,
    Lawrence, 17
Urbonas, John, 122
U.S. Post Office, 21, 22, 93
USO, 30, 35

V

Vaitkunas, A., 105
Veckys, A., 105
Veroneau, Ada, 51
Venti, Robert, 60
Verville, Ronald, 104
Verville, Thomas, 104
Villickas, A., 105
Vincent, Harold, 25
Vitale, Emil, 25
Vizinni, Jimmie, 73
Vizinni, Julia, 73
Vogel, Oswald W., 105
Volpe, John, 114, 127
Vose, Elliot, 79
Voyeur, Lorraine, 125

W

Waco Cabin biplane, 15
Wall, William X., 122
Walolis, John, 89
Walsh, Cheryl, 126
Walsh, Francis E., 123
Walsh, Mary E., 123
Walsh, Thomas, 126
Walsh's General Store, Plaistow,
    123
War Bond effort, 6, 14, 21, 22
Ward, Patricia, 129
Ward, Pete, 67
Warfield, Rev. Homer, 110
Washington Monument, Methuen,
    95, 104
Water Street fire, Haverhill, 88
Watson, Dorothy, 84
Watson, John, 84
Waverly Playground, North
    Andover, 80, 81
Webb, Joanne, 125
Webb, John, 125
Webber, Claire, 79

Weinman, Miss, 60
Wescott, Bertha, 60
Wessell, Bertha, 73
Western Electric Convention, North
    Andover, 116
White, Philip J., 134
White Rose Laundry employees,
    Methuen, 126
Whiteneck, Gigi, 100
Wiers Beach Ballroom, 103
Wills, Eileen, 132
Wilson, Evelyn, 51
Wilson, Ray, 60
Wilson, Stewart, 25
Windham Center School students,
    24
Winn, Jimmy, 101
Winslow, Minton A., 134
Winter, Harold, 73
Witkas, Walter, 105
Witworth, Herald, 66
Woekel, Ruth, 73
Wojnar, Mary, 78
Wolfendale, Peggy, 78
Woloshin, Stephen, 84
Wolvius, John, 80
Wood Mill presentations, 10
World War I Auditorium, Andover,
    32
World War I Veterans, 134
World War II
    about, 7
    Punchard High School W.W.II
        veterans class, 39
    scrap metal drive, 23
    soldiers, 14, 15, 22, 26
    statue dedication on Lawrence
        Common, 49
    USO Junior hostesses,
        Lawrence, 35
    War Bond effort, 6, 14, 21, 22
W.T. Grant Building, Haverhill, 42
W.T. Grant Store, Haverhill, 130
Wunderlich, Eddie, 64

Y

YMCA building campaign,
    Haverhill, 72
YMCA, Lawrence, 10, 30
Young, Richard, 104
Young, Willie, 73

Z

Zarwell, Margorie, 73
Zarzour, Paula, 125
Zraket, Charles, 12